The Meaning of
God's Providence

The MEANING of GOD'S PROVIDENCE
In Our Lives

by

Roberto de Mattei

Translated by Lucas Dube

SOPHIA INSTITUTE PRESS
Manchester, New Hampshire

Sophia Institute Press
Box 5284, Manchester, NH 03108
1-800-888-9344
www.SophiaInstitute.com

Sophia Institute Press is a registered trademark of Sophia Institute.

paperback ISBN 978-1-64413-955-4

ebook ISBN 978-1-64413-956-1

Library of Congress Control Number: 2023944877

Contents

PART TWO
The Sacred Order of the Universe

PART THREE
Disorder and Its Meaning

The Meaning of
God's Providence

Preface

Pax omnium rerum, tranquillitas ordinis
(Peace of all things, tranquility of order)
St. Augustine, *De Civitate Dei*, 19, 13

ALL THAT EXISTS HAS meaning, has a reason for being, and has a cause, and nothing that happens is removed from God, He who not only created the universe, but keeps it in existence and orders it to its ultimate end.

This — before even faith — common sense, philosophy, and natural theology tell us. It holds true for inanimate beings, from the smallest particles of matter to the stars of the sky. It applies to the affairs of peoples, nations, and civilizations.

There exists a supreme order, which is the arrangement of the universe according to the plans of Divine Providence, but there also exists a radical disorder, which is the attempt of the free creature to dismantle the divine order. This attempt is always destined to fail because, as St. Paul teaches us, in God's plans, all things work together toward the good: *Omnia cooperantur in bonum* (Rom. 8:28).

The confusion that we are immersed in today is worse than that of other eras, such as the barbarian invasions. Indeed, then the chaos was bloody and dramatically visible to every human eye. Today, the chaos is overwhelmingly of the moral, cultural, and spiritual orders, and the Catholic Church herself, which after the fall of the Roman Empire ensured the transition to a new, shining civilization, seems to be pervaded internally by a deep crisis.

The loss of souls is graver than the loss of life under the threat of wars, epidemics, and hunger, which once again looms over the world. But today, as in the past, radical disorder is opposed by Divine Providence, which is the manifestation of the glory of God in the created universe.

The diabolical plan to unravel the world and to make society return to the primordial darkness seems close to its realization, but through the Holy Spirit, who guides history,

God will once more bring about an order far higher than the depths of this contemporary pandemonium.

The following pages seek to be an act of great trust in the role that Divine Providence continues to play without fail in our lives and in the history of all mankind.

Roberto de Mattei
June 16, 2022
Feast of Corpus Christi

PART ONE

The Surrender to Divine Providence and the Triumph of the Immaculate Heart

1. Everything That Exists Has Meaning

In the created world, everything is guided by Providence because nothing is devoid of divine causality: *Nihil in terra sine causa fit* (Job 5:6). These words of Sacred Scripture express the sacred and providential order of the universe. Everything that exists and happens in the world has a cause and a meaning. "Nothing," reiterates St. Augustine, "occurs in the world by chance."[1] Everything has in God its exemplar cause, its efficient cause, and its final cause.

If God is the first cause of the universe, the beginning and ultimate end of all things, the highest archetype upon which all is modeled, nothing can escape His power and reign. Everything that exists has been created by Him,

---

[1] St. Augustine, *De diversis quaestionibus*, LXXXIII, liber unus, c. XXXIV.

loved by Him, directed to its end by Him. Every being and movement in the universe is gathered in the invisible hands of Divine Providence. The providential order is sacred because everything comes from God, and everything is related to Him.

"All things, even the very smallest, are placed under Divine Providence," St. Thomas firmly states.[2] The order of Divine Providence extends to every sphere of creation, to the smallest of details. This does not impoverish God, but rather it constitutes proof of His greatness. It is precisely because God is infinite that He can occupy Himself with the smallest details of creation without being diminished by it. God is not ambivalent to what belongs to Him, and nothing in the universe is absent His sovereignty.

To an infinite Being, there is nothing great or small, because He is the cause of being for all things. "Nothing is too big nor too small for the Infinite," writes Fr. Dohet, "nothing absorbs Him, nothing fills Him, nothing surpasses Him."[3] If anything, however small and insignificant, could escape Divine Providence, the omnipotence of God would

---

[2] St. Thomas Aquinas, *Compendium Theologiae*, cap. 154, n. 308. Cfr. ivi I, cap. 130, n. 262.

[3] Paul Dohet S.J., *L'irréprochable Providence*, Desclée, Paris, 1954, p. 125.

be nullified and His infinite love would be obstructed. There would exist realities separate from Him, and He would cease to be the first and universal cause of every reality and perfection.

The mystery of Providence is that of a God who is not indifferent to that which He has created, but instead regards everything that concerns even the smallest creature, since "from Him and through Him and for Him are all things" (Rom. 11:36). If God cares for every minute detail of the universe, should it be even a grain of sand, what then should we think of His care for man, created in His image and likeness, in whom He Himself became incarnate? St. Augustine, regarding not only the fact that God cares about human affairs but also how great this care is, writes: "There is no greater and more reliable testimony than that offered by Christ the man: the manifestation of Christ who is born; the patience of Christ who dies; the power of Christ who rises again."[4]

Divine causality encompasses all outside of sin: nothing avoids it, neither free creatures nor irrational ones, neither events nor society. "Divine action," writes Fr. De Caussade, "floods the universe, seeps into every creature, filling them to

---

4   St. Augustine, *Discorso sulla Provvidenza*, cit., p. 35.

the brim with itself. Wherever they are, there it is; it precedes them; it accompanies them; it follows them."[5] The revelation of the glory of God is the ultimate goal of all divine action. For everything that God accomplishes tends, and cannot but tend, toward the revelation of His glory.

The movement by which God progresses the universe forward approximates the life of the universe and is attributed by the Angelic Doctor to the Holy Spirit.[6] From the very first moment of Creation, the continuous and uninterrupted action of the Holy Spirit accomplishes the divine will in the universe. God does not only preserve His creatures in their being, but acts upon them continuously through His grace, which governs the course of events imperceptibly: this constant and infallible rule over the creatures and things of the world has the name Divine Providence.

Divine Providence extends to every aspect of the universe. Nothing happens without the order or permission of God, from the rotation of the stars to the smallest movement of the smallest living beings. St. Thomas asserts that God is present in all creation through participation,

---

5   Jean-Pierre de Caussade, *L'abbandono alla Divina Provvidenza*, tr. Ital. Paoline, Cinisello Balsamo 1979, p. 33.

6   St. Thomas Aquinas, *Compendium Theologiae*, I, cap. 147, n. 295.

power, and essence, insofar as He is present in the innermost part of all things, giving them their being.[7] This formula, according to Fr. Fabro, "expresses in the highest culmination and with the greatest stillness of the Absolute lowered into the finite, the supreme dependence of the finite upon the infinite."[8]

2. Primary Causes and Secondary Causes of the Universe

All things tend in their actions toward the end which is constituted by divine goodness. "For this reason," writes St. Thomas, "all things are directed toward this end by the same God, whose own end this is. But this is proper to him who is ruled and governed by someone's providence: therefore all things are governed by Divine Providence."[9]

When we examine an inferior cause, what seems to be fortuitous or accidental with respect to an inferior cause, seeing as it occurs beyond the scope of its intention, is in fact neither fortuitous nor accidental with respect to a higher cause, as it is not brought about outside of its intention. "This

---

[7] Id., *Super Evang. S. Ioannis Lec.*, I, 8; *Compendium Theologiae*, I, cap. 135.

[8] Cornelio Fabro, *Esegesi tomistica*, Pontificia Università Lateranense, Roma 1969, p. 466.

[9] St. Thomas Aquinas, *Compendium Theologiae*, I, cap. 123, n. 240.

is clear, for example, in the case of the master who sends two servants to the same place, such that each is unaware of the other: their encounter is by chance for both of them, but not for the master who sent them."[10]

Chance does not exist. There are what seem to be accidents and unexpected mishaps, but they only appear as such to us and not to the Providence which foresees them and orders them to the common good of the universe. These accidents happen thanks to the confluence of many causes, each of which produces its own effect such that by their interaction an altogether different nature results, which all the causes have contributed to but none could have foreseen. All apparent accidents, whether in the physical world or among humans, are contained within the hands of Divine Providence.[11] "Providence," writes St. Francis de Sales, "pertains to everything, it reigns over it all, and it leads everything back to its own glory."[12]

God, the first and highest cause of the universe, works through secondary causes that He weaves together and directs toward the same end. All the effects of these causes can be attributed to God, according to St. Thomas, just as the

[10] Ibid., cap. 137, n. 278.

[11] Id., *Summa Theologiae*, I, q. 116, a. 1 resp.

[12] St. Francis de Sales, *Trattato dell'Amor di Dio*, pp. 184–85.

work that is accomplished by an instrument is attributed to the artist.[13] "The causes of all events," writes the Venerable Lessius, "are held and chained by His hand in such a way that without a sign of His will, none of these could be freed from its chain to produce an act."[14] The web of causality envelops and sustains the universe, giving it meaning.

Everything that participates in the divine causality is a secondary cause of the universe. Secondary causes can be rational and irrational creatures, angels, men, events, and all the possible influences that can contribute to the development of creatures. Through these secondary causes at every moment and in every circumstance of our existence, God takes action in a profound and invisible way upon us, with the supernatural influence that most befits us. He sets earth and Heaven in motion, moving indetectable elements and intelligent causes to influence us and guide us toward our end.

The organization of these causes is not egalitarian, but hierarchical. God, explains the Angelic Doctor, governs the lower beings through the higher ones, not because He cannot manage them directly, but to generously share the dignity of causality with those higher

[13] St. Thomas Aquinas, *Compendium Theologiae*, I, cap. 135, n. 274.
[14] L. Lessius, *Les noms divins*, cit., p. 118.

creatures.[15] Since creatures of intellect are higher than the others, it is clear, writes St. Thomas, that the other creatures are governed by God through these intellectual creatures.[16]

"For this reason," explains St. Thomas, "men, who rank lowest among the intellectual substances according to the order of their nature, are governed by higher spirits who, by virtue of the fact that they bring to men messages of divine matters, are called angels, i.e., messengers. And the lower angels are in turn governed by higher angels according to the different hierarchies, that is principalities, by which they are distinguished, and which are distinguished within the individual hierarchies by different orders."[17]

The fact that God acts through creatures, notes Fr. Nicolas, does not at all diminish His role in anything. On the contrary, not only does He will and act, but He causes them to will and act: "He causes beings to participate not only in what He is but also in what He does; not only in His being and action, but His thought and love: in His Providence."[18]

[15]   St. Thomas Aquinas, *Summa Theologiae*, I, q. 22, a. 3.

[16]   Id., *Compendium Theologiae*, I, cap. 125, n. 245.

[17]   Ibid., n. 246; *Summa Theologiae*, I, q. 106, a. 1.

[18]   J. M. Nicolas, *La Provvidenza*, cit., p. 111.

3. The Angels, Instruments of Divine Providence

Angels are the preeminent of the secondary causes. These, says St. Thomas, have as their assignment "the implementation of Divine Providence with regard to men."[19]

Angels are pure spirits, infused with the Holy Spirit. As great as their number is, each of them has its own inimitable face. Their number exceeds that of any material creature: they are more numerous than the flowers in the fields, than snowflakes, than stars in the sky. According to Sacred Scripture they are "myriad" (Heb. 12:22; Rev. 7). But they are not equals: they form an angelic society divided in three hierarchies and nine choirs. According to St. Thomas, the first hierarchy is comprised of Seraphim, Cherubim, and Thrones; the second, Dominions, Virtues, and Powers; the third, Principalities, Archangels, and Angels. All realities of the universe, writes St. Augustine, are understood by the angels in the Word of God, "where they contemplate the causes and reasons according to which they were created, in their unchanging steadiness; and in a different way in themselves."[20]

Made to serve, the angel is not only contemplative but, *more suo*, has an active nature because it is an agent of the

---

[19] St. Thomas Aquinas, *Summa Theologiae*, I, q. 113, a. 2.

[20] St. Augustine, *De civitate Dei*, II, 29.

will of God in the direction of the universe.[21] St. Thomas asserts that "all physical things are governed by the angels."[22] This means that the angels govern all that is corporeal in the universe, from the microcosm of the atoms to the boundless and majestic world of the stars. They are the secondary causes of motion, light, life, and heat, as well as of those principle elements of the physical universe which suggest to man the notions of cause and effect.

Through the angels, God takes action on us in a profound and invisible manner at every moment and in every circumstance of our existence in order to guide us toward our supernatural end. It is for this reason that to every man, from the moment he is born, God assigns a guardian angel to protect and guide him. The angelic guardian is not taken from anyone alive, no matter how bad he may be. Only the damned are deprived of this.[23]

Angels are not, however, only instruments for the sanctification of individual souls. Where men gather in societies, where there are families, whether natural or spiritual, or where there are groups of families, such as

[21]   P. Corrêa de Oliveira, *A inocência primeva*, cit., p. 272.
[22]   St. Thomas Aquinas, *Summa theologiae*, I, q. 110, a. 1.
[23]   Francesco Eiximenis, *Il libro degli Angeli* (1392), tr. Ital. Gribaudi, Milano 2000, pp. 150–53.

nations, there too are angels, the instruments of the glory, even the public glory, of God. For this reason, there are angels of nations, angels of peoples, angels of the Church. St. Thomas, who is called the "Angelic Doctor" precisely for his teaching on the angels, about whom he dwells in many works, most of all in the *Summa Theologiae*, adds that the guardianship of human collectives is the responsibility of the angelic order of principalities, or perhaps archangels.[24]

The mission of the angels regarding nations is above all their protection and temporal assistance. For this reason, in Deuteronomy it is said that "When the Most High allotted each nation its heritage, when he separated out human beings, He set up the boundaries of the peoples after the number of the angels of God" (Deut. 32:8).[25]

The angels are in the presence of God (Isa. 6:2) to whom they offer unending worship (Rev. 4:5); they connect Heaven and earth, participate in the events of history, and come to the aid of men, peoples, and the Church.

[24] St. Thomas Aquinas, *Summa Theologiae*, I, q. 113, a. 3, resp.
[25] The author cites this verse of Deuteronomy according to the Greek version of the Pentateuch (according to the number of the angels of God) and not according to the more well-known Hebrew version (according to the number of the sons of Israel).–Translator.

The universe is governed by angels, present in every moment and every place as instruments of Divine Providence, messengers of graces, protagonists and witnesses of divine plans. We read in Revelation that St. John saw all the angels singing the divine glory: "Holy, holy, holy is the Lord God almighty, who was, and who is, and who is to come" (Rev. 4:8).

4. All That Happens Is the Will of God

Everything is Providence because everything is the divine will. Nothing happens that God neither wills nor permits. "Everything that happens in the world occurs only for the good of the souls subject to the will of God."[26]

As St. Thomas explains, the will of God, no different from His Intellect,[27] is the first rule of the order of creation for all rational creatures.[28] This, in the words of Fr. Vital Lehodey, "is the universal principle of being, life, and action: all occurs in accordance with His will, and nothing happens apart from what it wills; there is no effect that does not derive from this first cause, nor movement that does not

---

[26] J.-P. de Caussade, *L'abbandono alla Divina Provvidenza*, cit., p. 174.

[27] St. Thomas Aquinas, *Compendium Theologiae*, I, c. 33, n. 65.

[28] Id., *Summa Theologiae*, II–IIae, q. 104, a. 1, ad 2.

originate from this first mover."[29] As a result, there are not occurrences, big or small, that do not manifest to us the will to which we must submit. "Even the hairs of your head have all been counted," the divine teacher reminds us, "Yet not one of them falls without your Father's will" (Matt. 6:25–34; 10:29–31).

The divine will reveals in two ways to man what theologians define as the will of expression and the will of good pleasure.

The will of expression is manifested in a direct manner through objective laws or rules, such as God's commandments and the doctrine of the Church, the advice and inspirations we receive, the duties inherent in our condition and all that "expresses" to us, i.e., reveals to us, what we must do. This is enclosed in the words of Scripture: "Fear God and keep his commandments, for this concerns all humankind" (Eccles. 12:13).

Man must conform himself to the will of expression of God, observing above all else His eternal and immutable law, which is expressed in the Decalogue and in the doctrine of the Church, according to the example of the divine teacher: "I have kept my Father's commandments and remain in his

---

[29] Dom Vital Lehodey, *Il santo abbandono*, tr. Ital. Paoline, Cinisello Balsamo 2014, p. 28.

love" (John 15:10). Every Christian dogma is a law because it obligates those whom it enlightens, and every law, notes Msgr. Gay, is itself a dogma because it enlightens those whom it obligates.[30] The law is therefore the flame that illuminates the life of the faithful, according to the words of Scripture: "For the commandment is a lamp, and the law is a light" (Prov. 6:23).

The Decalogue, the law engraved by God, is the basis of the objective order of creation and the foundation of all civil coexistence, the exemplary form upon which the conduct of men and peoples is to be modeled, the divine light burning to guide and enlighten them.

The duties of the state, which are higher than particular duties because they are directly ordered to the common good, fall under the will of expression. "The good order of the world," writes St. Claude la Colombière, "depends on the fidelity of each person to accomplish their own duties to the state. All disorders arise from negligence in fulfilling them."[31] He who neglects his own duties does not only condemn himself, but also compromises the salvation of his neighbor.

---

[30] Mons. Carlo Gay, *Vita e virtù cristiane considerate nello stato religioso*, tr. Ital. Editrice Gregoriana, Padova 1937, vol. II, p. 340.

[31] St. Claude la Colombière, *Il libro dell'interiorità. Scritti spirituali*, Città Nuova, Roma 1992, p. 228.

The will of good pleasure instead presents itself through facts and events that do not depend on our will. The senses do not discern anything beyond the action of the creature, but this, as Fr. Cassaude observes, "is a veil which covers the profound mysteries of divine action.... If we were to pierce the veil and if we were vigilant and attentive, God would reveal Himself to us unceasingly and we would enjoy His presence in all that happens to us; at each thing we would say: *Dominus est*, It is the Lord!"[32]

Everything that happens in us and around us contains divine action. It shows up in all that God gives us, but also in all that He takes from us for our own good. God can take away our health and life; He can deprive us of riches, of the reputation and honors we aspire to; He can take away our dearest affections: everything, except the hope that we can and should always harbor in Him.

The will of good pleasure is therefore what we must recognize in adversity, in prosperity, and in all circumstances that happen within us and outside of us, without depending upon us. The words of St. Paul sum up the meaning: "All things work for good for those who love God" (Rom. 8:28).

---

[32] J.-P. de Caussade, *L'abbandono alla Divina Provvidenza*, cit., pp. 168–169.

God is no different from His will, and the will of God must be the singular and highest rule of human action, even social action. Man, in imitation of God, must also learn the skill of how to derive good from the bad that happens against his will, according to the divine calling that is a blueprint for life: "Do not be conquered by evil but conquer evil with good" (Rom. 12:21).

5. Surrender to Divine Providence

We must be convinced that "what happens to us at every moment by order of God is the holiest, most fitting, and most divine thing that exists for us."[33] The saints, theologians, and spiritual masters define union of man's will with that of God as an act of perfect charity. For true charity consists in love of God; but since love consists first of all in doing the will of the beloved, there is no act of charity higher or more perfect for a creature than to fully conform its will to the divine will. "God and His will are the eternal goal which captivates the heart in a state of faith, and which in that of glory will make its true happiness."[34] In this properly lies the surrender to Divine Providence, which is the supreme act of love, a synthesis of theological and cardinal virtues, defined by St. Francis de Sales as "virtue

[33] Ibid., p. 98.
[34] Ibid., p. 69.

of virtues, chrism of charity, scent of humility, merit of patience, and fiat of perseverance"[35] and by Fr. Cassaude: "a mixture of faith, hope, and charity in a single act that unites the heart to God and to His action."[36] No road is better than this to scale the summits of the interior life. In this sense, as St. Alphonsus Liguori says, uniting our will to the will of God "is the height of perfection."[37]

Man's perfection consists in conforming himself to the will of God, or rather in doing His glory, for in the glory of God the will of man and the divine will find their perfect and singular harmony. The human will, feeble and fickle, must therefore conform itself to its divine counterpart which neither bends nor changes. In it, the vocation of the rational creature is fulfilled. The vocation of every soul is constituted by what God asks of it; it is the special form within which Providence wants each person to work and develop. Every man has a particular vocation because he was willed and loved by God in a different manner. There are no two identical creatures nor, in the course of history, have there ever been two absolutely identical, because the

---

[35] St. Francis de Sales, *Trattenimenti*, cit., p. 64.

[36] J.-P. de Caussade, *L'abbandono alla Divina Provvidenza*, cit., p. 71.

[37] St. Alphonsus Liguori, *Uniformità alla volontà di Dio*, Padri Redentoristi, Bussolengo 1987, p. 9.

will of God is different for every creature, and every creature, which has emerged from nothingness into time, is unrepeatable. This vocation, writes Fr. Faber, springs directly from our eternal predestination, but is entrusted to the hands of our free will and depends upon it.[38] There is no other road that leads man to the holiness that each man is called to be happy.

God has placed an angel near to us to watch over our vocation. Our guardian angel is our fulfilled vocation, our vocation realized. He is the model of our vocation. For this reason we must pray to him and listen to the words that he murmurs to us.

"We must surrender ourselves to the will of God," warns Cardinal Merry del Val, "because the will and the love of God are one and the same thing; they are the basis of the dispositions of Divine Providence."[39] "This," writes Fr. Nicolas, "was, one can say, the very spirituality of Jesus, when He was on earth, which radiated from Him and which He preached":[40] "I do not seek my own will but the will of the one who sent me" (John 5:30). The

---

[38] Frederick W. Faber, *Conferenze spirituali*, tr. Ital. Pietro Marietti, Torino 1871, p. 381.

[39] Card. Raffaele Merry del Val, *Pensieri ascetici*, a cura della Postulazione, Roma 1953, p. 75.

[40] J. M. Nicolas, *La Provvidenza*, cit., p. 142.

dramatic scene at Gethsemane shows us how closely this communion of His human will with that divine will of the Father was joined, and the Savior's very words express it: "My Father, if it is possible, let this cup pass from me; yet, not as I will, but as you will" (Matt. 26:39). "Man," writes Msgr. Landucci, "insofar as he is called moment to moment to say 'yes' to the divine will, is for this reason himself called to perfectly and therefore heroically enact virtue: he is called to heroic holiness."[41] The call to perfect and heroic sanctity is universal because this is the will of God. His infinite mercy assures us of the possibility to reach this goal. Everything that happens in our lives, independent of our will, is ordered to our happiness and to His glory.

Our life, in this sense, must be a continuous offering and continuous thanksgiving for all that the will of God reveals to us. The spirit of thanksgiving, reminds Fr. Faber, has been the characteristic spirit of the saints in every age.[42]

The words *Deo gratias*, repeated in every circumstance of our lives, express our surrender to Divine Providence.

---

[41] Mons. Pier Carlo Landucci, *La sacra vocazione*, Edizioni Paoline, Roma 1955, p. 25.

[42] F. W. Faber, *Tutto per Gesù, ovvero gli agevoli modi d'amore divino*, tr. Ital. Pietro Marietti, Torino 1868, p. 266.

6. Cooperation with the Will of God

Surrender to Divine Providence is the secret of holiness, as St. Alphonsus Liguori teaches us, because "all holiness consists in loving God and the love of God consists in fulfilling His will. This is our life. '*Et vita in voluntate eius*' (Ps. 30:6)."[43] Fr. Garrigou-Lagrange expresses the doctrine of surrender in this principle: "Nothing happens that God has not foreseen from all eternity and that He has not willed or at least permitted."[44] Not only has God foreseen from all eternity what is and will be, but He has willed what is good in those events, and as regards evil and disorder, He has only permitted them. To this principle, there follows another: God cannot will anything nor permit anything except in view of what He has set out to create, that is to say in view of the manifestation of His goodness, His infinite perfections, and the glory of the God-Man, Jesus Christ, His only Son. As St. Paul asserts: "All belong to you, and you to Christ, and Christ to God" (1 Cor. 3:23). "This submission to the will of God," writes St. Claude la Colombière, "frees us from every burden. For, since God wills everything that happens

---

[43] St. Alphonsus Liguori, *Regolamento di vita*, Paoline, Cinisello Balsamo 1986, p. 72.

[44] R. Garrigou-Lagrange, O.P., *La Providence et la confiance en Dieu*, Les Editions Militia, Montréal 1953, p. 232.

to us, and we will all that God wants, there is nothing that happens to us except that which we will."[45] They who have understood the mystery of Providence end up not willing anything but what God wills for them.

Surrender to Divine Providence does not only consist in accepting everything that does not depend on the will of men as willed by God, but also and above all, in ordering toward Him, the first principle, everything that directly depends on the human will.

This surrender does not exempt us from doing what we can to fulfill the will of God shown to us by commandments, council, and circumstance. "God does not want us to fall asleep in inactivity," explains Fr. de Saint Laurent, "He acts that we might imitate Him. His most perfect activity is without limits: He is pure act. We therefore must act; but we must only expect the success of our actions to come from Him."[46] St. Ignatius also states, "In everything that you must do, this is the rule of rules to follow: Trust in God, acting as if the success of each thing depended entirely upon you and not at all on God; but while employing your efforts toward the good result, do not rely on

---

[45]   St. Claude la Colombière, *Il libro dell'interiorità*, cit., p. 368.

[46]   Thomas de Saint Laurent, *Il libro della fiducia*, Ed. Fiducia, Roma 1991, p. 28.

them and proceed as if everything must have been done by God alone and nothing by you."[47]

Surrender to Divine Providence is not then passivity and inaction, but the active cooperation of the human will with the divine will. Nothing is farther away from the true Christian than the fatalist. The latter is defeated and discouraged, while the former fights with that joy that is born of deep trust in God.

Man, composed of body and soul, is endowed with the faculty that allows him to understand, to will, to act, i.e., to accomplish what his will loves as good and true. In the capability of man to do God's will as a consequence of the gift of freedom lies the difference between rational creatures and those beings devoid of reason. "By the Lord's word his works were brought into being; he accepts the one who does his will" (Sir. 42:15). The beings without reason conform themselves to the divine will by physical necessity, without the ability to shirk from it. Rational creatures are free to unite their will to the divine will, reciprocating the love that is the cause of their being. This orientation toward God is an essential good not only of every single creature but also of society and the entire universe, as considered

---

[47]   R. P. Xavier de Franciosi, *L'Esprit de saint Ignace*, Le Chevallier, Nancy 1887, p. 5.

within time and space, and of history in its entirety as the product of human events.[48]

And this is the teaching of the Sermon on the Mount: "Look at the birds in the sky; they do not sow or reap, they gather nothing into barns, yet your heavenly Father feeds them. Are not you more important than they? Learn from the way the wild flowers grow. They do not work or spin. But I tell you that not even Solomon in all his splendor was clothed like one of them" (Matt. 6:26, 28–29). "So do not worry and say, 'What are we to eat?' or 'What are we to drink?' or 'What are we to wear?' All these things the pagans seek. Your heavenly Father knows that you need them all. But seek first the kingdom [of God] and his righteousness, and all these things will be given you besides" (Matt. 6:31–33).

The last sentence, it can be said, summarizes the evangelical theology of Divine Providence. For this reason, Pius XII affirms that "there is a rock in this world, placed by Christ; upon this rock, one must stand and turn his sight on high; from there the restoration of all things in Christ finds its source. Now, Christ has revealed the secret of it: '*Quaerite primum regnum Dei et iustitiam eius, et haec omnia adicientur vobis*' (Matt. 6:33)."[49]

---

48   St. Thomas Aquinas, *Contra Gentiles*, III, c. 69.

49   Pius XII, Address to the Roman Aristocracy, January 16, 1946.

7. Faithfulness in Small Things

If even the smallest particle of matter has its own reason and meaning and participates in the divine plan of the universe, imagine the value of a human act produced by the rational creature, which is not compelled but free.

St. Paul writes in the First Letter to the Corinthians: "So whether you eat or drink, or whatever you do, do everything for the glory of God" (10:31); and in the Letter to the Colossians he reiterates: "And whatever you do, in word or in deed, do everything in the name of the Lord" (3:17). Every human act dependent upon the deliberation of reason, states St. Thomas, is, in its individuality, good or bad.[50] Everything that is the fruit of the free will of man can and must tend toward the good and is aimed toward the Divine Maker. What makes the value of a human act immeasurable is the fact that it can be ordered toward God and participate in the divine goodness and perfection.

In this sense, there is no human act dependent on reason and will that is in itself insignificant or unimportant. Man, in the course of time, makes the same choice that the angels made in the span of an instant at the moment of their creation. In every word, thought, and action — even the

---

[50] St. Thomas Aquinas, *Summa Theologiae*, I–IIae, q. 18, a. 9.

very smallest — he is called to contribute to the divine plan of the universe. All the acts of man in time, even the littlest, have weight in eternity. The smallest meritorious act is worth more than any material reality because it causes us to grow in grace, and grace, which is participation in the divine nature, has immeasurable value in comparison to the greatest earthly goods.

Therefore, perfection should be sought out even and above all in the littlest things, in imitation of our Father, who is perfect in Heaven (Matt. 5:48). This teaching, as Fr. Garrigou-Lagrange explains, is very consoling because it follows from it that "in the life of the just man every deliberate act that is not a sin is, at the same time, morally good and meritorious, whether it is easy or difficult, large or small."[51]

The Gospel teaches that he who is faithful in the small things is also faithful in great things (Luke 16:10), and Fr. Surin explains that "perfection shines more in the little things than in the great things because man is drawn to great things by a momentary impulse, while the perfect

---

[51] R. Garrigou-Lagrange, O.P., *La Providence et la confiance en Dieu*, cit., p. 263.

good is seen within ordinary things."[52] "The little things," asserts St. Augustine, "are little things, but to be faithful in these is a great thing."[53]

The "little things" form the fabric of man's duties. All perfection of the Christian life is in the mysterious balance between active faithfulness to his daily duty and trustful surrender to divine grace, which manifests itself in the unexpected events that each moment of the day brings us. "This union of faithfulness and surrender," Fr. Garrigou-Lagrange rightly observes, "gives us a glimpse of what must be the union of asceticism, which insists on fidelity or conformity to the will of God, and of mysticism, which puts the emphasis on surrender."[54] This is "God's wisdom, mysterious [and] hidden," that St. Paul speaks of (1 Cor. 1:6).

A perfect example of surrender to Divine Providence and of supreme excellence in the faithful fulfillment of his own stately duty was St. Joseph, the most chaste husband of the Mother of God and foster father of Jesus, to whom God entrusted the Holy Family and the entire Church.

---

[52] Jean-Joseph Surin, *Guida spirituale alla perfezione*, tr. Ital. Paoline, Cinisello Balsamo (Milano) 1988, l. 2, p. 78.

[53] St. Augustine, *De doctrina christiana*, IV, 18, 35.

[54] R. Garrigou-Lagrange O.P., *La Providence et la confiance en Dieu*, cit., p. 237.

8. The Duty of the Present Moment

God's mark in the universe is not only present in every particle created that subsists stably in being, but in every created moment that flows forth in its unfolding. Even time is a creature, and every moment can be understood as an event or a set of events with its own character and unity. For every finite reality, including time, receives its being from the creative and preserving act of God. "This act is singular, infinite, and eternal; it encompasses the totality of its unfolding," writes Fr. Nicolas. "God is not the first among the beings that He creates, He moves and develops; He is 'during.' He does not foresee, but sees; He is present to everything that is and coexists with everyone to whom He gives being and with each of their moments."[55] There is no instant in time, just as there is not point in space, that is devoid of the fullness of the divine action that floods the universe.

It is up to man to recognize or refuse this divine presence in the present moment. "The present moment," notes Fr. Caussade, "is always full of infinite treasures; it contains more than you can possibly take in."[56] The duty of every moment, underneath appearances which are often modest, Fr. Garrigou-Lagrange adds, contains the expression of the will of God

---

[55] J. M. Nicolas, *La Provvidenza*, cit., p. 66.

[56] J.-P. de Caussade, *L'abbandono alla Divina Provvidenza*, cit., p. 132.

for us and our individual lives.[57] The present moment, writes Canon Feige, "is indeed always like an ambassador who brings to us the order of God, to whom everything is a means, everything is an instrument of sanctification of His elect."[58] All saints have lived the spirituality of the present moment, fulfilling the divine will as manifested to them from hour to hour, moment to moment, without letting themselves be disconcerted by unforeseen setbacks and without focusing on their future. "Their secret was to live from moment to moment what divine action wished for them to do."[59]

In his *Spiritual Diary*, St. Claude la Colombière outlined this plan: "To live day by day. To hope to die in the occupation we perform."[60] In short, to seek perfection in the present moment, according to ancient adage *age quod agis*: "Do well what you are doing." For his part, Cardinal Merry del Val writes, "Let us often reflect that there is no moment of the day nor circumstance in our life that is not permitted or willed by God so that we may use it to demonstrate our love to Him."[61]

---

[57] R. Garrigou-Lagrange, O.P., *La Providence et la confiance en Dieu*, cit., p. 255.

[58] Canonico Pierre Feige, *Santifichiamo il momento presente*, Edizioni Fiducia, Roma 2021, p. 9.

[59] Ibid., p. 256.

[60] St. Claude la Colombière, *Il libro dell'interiorità*, cit., p. 69.

[61] R. Merry del Val, *Pensieri ascetici*, cit., p. 44.

Surrender to Divine Providence means fulfillment of God's will moment by moment, especially when it manifests itself in the form of tribulations and the cross, without worrying about tomorrow. A short verse of the Gospel sums up this philosophy of life and this profound supernatural spirit: "Sufficient for a day is its own evil" (Matt. 6:34).

Surrender, then, is nothing less than perfect submission to order of God according to the demands of the present moment. "In surrender," writes Fr. Caussade, "the only rule comes to us from the present moment."[62] Father Garrigou-Lagrange explains how we must not limit ourselves to seeing the present moment on the horizontal axis of time, between a past that is no more and a future that is not yet. "We live above all," he writes, "upon the vertical line that connects it to the one instant of motionless eternity. Come what may, we say: at this moment God is and wants to draw me to Him."[63]

Nevertheless, divine eternity does not consist in a succession of moments: it is the singular and infinite instant, an ever-contemporary totality. Providence is an eternal act by which God leads His creatures through historical time. The appearance of the incarnate Word on earth is the climax of all human

[62] J. P. de Caussade, *L'abbandono alla Divina Provvidenza*, cit., p. 61.

[63] R. Garrigou-Lagrange O.P., *La Providence et la confiance en Dieu*, cit., p. 269.

history. "Before Jesus Christ there were many centuries of waiting; after Jesus Christ there is a span of time whose secret is unknown to man because no man knows the hour of the birth of the last chosen; and it is for the chosen, for whom the Son of God became incarnate, that the world is preserved."[64]

9. The Divine Kingship over the Universe

Just as no human act is morally insignificant because every deliberate act has its measure and reference in God, so too there is no act performed by man that is devoid of public and social consequences because man was created to live in society and all that man does has its measure in the good of God and the good of his neighbor. For man has a relationship of order not only to God, but also toward all other creatures, beginning with those closest to him. There is an affiliation of man with man, which begins from the moment of his conception, just as there is a partnership of man with God, which begins in time through grace and is fulfilled in eternity through glory.[65]

Man is by nature social because his nature as a created being inclines him to receive good from others and to communicate to others the perfection that is his own, that is, the

---

64   Dom Prosper Guéranger, *Il senso cristiano della storia*, tr. Ital. Il Falco, Milano 1982, pp. 15–16.

65   St. Thomas Aquinas, *Summa Theologiae*, I–IIae, q. 65, a. 5.

good that he himself receives from divine goodness. God is the common good of every man and every human society.[66] Human society is the collection of rational beings called to participate in the divine plan. Created in the image and likeness of God, who is the supreme good, and participating in the divine good he receives from God, man is called to spread and communicate it beyond himself. Society can be defined as the place where souls communicate to one another the good they have received from Divine Providence.

The Kingdom of God is also social, because God created man so that he might live in association with his fellow human beings, and human society has an end which is no different from that of each man individually considered. Man is born in society, lives in society, and contributes with his every act to determine the life of society. "It is a miserly goodness that thinks only of itself and its own soul," writes Fr. Faber.[67] Man, insofar as he is a social being, is ordered to the common good of society which is more perfect than the singular good of the individual. The good of a community, says the Angelic Doctor, taking up Aristotle, "is superior to the good of an individual who belongs to it."[68] The good of society is no different from

[66] Ibid., q. 109, a. 3.
[67] F. W. Faber, *Tutto per Gesu*, cit., p. 133.
[68] St. Thomas Aquinas, *Summa Theologiae*, II–IIae, q. 39, a. 2, ad 2.

the good of the men who make it up or from the good of the whole universe: the glory of God. But it achieves this end via the common good of its members: a good "that is the end of individual people who live in a community," writes St. Thomas, "like the good of the whole is the end of each of its parts."[69]

"The great law of history," writes Fr. Ramière, "that is, the highest objective proposed by the divine will to individuals, societies, and all of humanity is the establishment of the Kingdom of Christ. By the Kingdom of Christ, we mean the perfect likeness and complete submission of individuals, peoples, and all humanity to the Man-God, sovereign model of all perfections and sovereign Lord of all things."[70]

There is no such thing as purely human or secular history, because everything that is created including time and the passing of the centuries is caused by God and ordered by Him. "Man," notes Dom Guéranger, "is called by God to a supernatural destiny; this is his end. The history of humanity must testify to this."[71] "History," writes Fr. Calmel, "is granted to the Church in order to make explicit

---

[69] Ibid., q. 58, a. 9, ad 3.

[70] Henri Ramière S.J., *O Reino de Jesus Cristo na História. Introdução ao estudo da teologia da História*, Civilização, Porto 2001, p. 185.

[71] Dom Guéranger, *Il senso cristiano della storia*, cit., p. 9.

the definitive riches of grace and truth that the Lord has deposited within it."[72]

The end of history is no different from the end of man: the Kingdom of Jesus Christ in souls and in societies.

10. Revolution and Counter-Revolution

The pursuit of God's glory is all the more perfect the deeper and greater its scope extends. There is no greater glory of God on earth than His social glory destined to be expressed in the historical triumph of the Church and Christian civilization. Christian civilization is the daughter of the Church and, like the Church, springs from the divine blood of Jesus Christ shed on Calvary. It is the earthly mirror of the divine order of the universe and represents the highest good that the human creature can produce corresponding to divine grace. The struggle for its establishment is the highest active expression of man's cooperation with Divine Providence.

God is "King of kings and Lord of lords" (1 Tim. 6:15). The Kingdom of God is to be sought first of all in our soul, but then it is to be extended and radiated out around us, so that it permeates the entire society, Christianizing it. Christian civilization is the realization on earth of that true peace

---

[72] R. T. Calmel, O.P., *Teologia della storia*, cit., p. 77.

which St. Augustine calls "the tranquility of order."[73] The denial of Christian civilization is revolution understood as disorder par excellence.

"And by order," writes Plinio Corrêa de Oliveira, "we mean the peace of Christ within the Kingdom of Christ. That is, the austere and hierarchical Christian civilization, fundamentally sacred, anti-egalitarian and anti-liberal."[74] Christian civilization is austere because it is as pure as the Immaculate Church by which it is shaped; it is hierarchical because it assigns its place to everything; it is sacred because everything points to God; it is anti-egalitarian because it suppresses every manifestation of pride; it is anti-liberal because it does not give concessions to disordered freedom or compromise between light and darkness. Plinio Corrêa de Oliveira, like Donoso Cortés and so many leaders of Christian thought, calls revolution the denial of Christian society and counter-revolution the restoration of the order that the revolutionary process denies.

In this sense, to react against the sin of revolution, which aims to take away from God the public glory that is owed to Him, is the human act that best seems to fulfill the divine teacher's words, "But seek first the kingdom [of God]

73   St. Augustine, *De Civitate Dei*, lib. 19, c. 13, 1.
74   P. Corrêa de Oliveira, *Rivoluzione e Contro-Rivoluzione*, cit., p. 103.

and his righteousness, and all these things will be given you besides" (Matt. 6:33; Luke 12:32).

To fight against revolution is to seek divine justice above all other interests, including spiritual ones. Nothing more selfless can be imagined than to neglect one's own interests in order to do only God's, and to do them not in relation to oneself, but for the common good of human society. In this common good lies the divine order of society, denied by the revolution. Every Christian, in this respect, is called to be a counter-revolutionary and to hate evil even more than the revolutionaries hate good. The Kingdom of God on earth, which anticipates and prefigures the heavenly one, is the noblest goal of a human heart.

Counter-revolution is also an action and movement, like the revolution it opposes. Its momentum, however, arises from good, is nourished at the sources of grace, and has the opposite characteristics to that of evil. The driving force of counter-revolution is in the faculties of the soul ordered and enlightened by grace. Grace, the supernatural principle of every good, the sanctifying influence of every action, gives to counter-revolution, as to every human action, its victorious impulse. Our Lady, mediator and distributor of all graces, is the necessary source of every authentic reaction to the revolution that threatens the Church and society. The goal of the counter-revolution is the restoration of Christian civilization, of which our Lady is Mother and Queen. Jesus Christ, King of Heaven and Earth, relinquished sovereignty of it to Mary, Co-Redemptrix of the human race and Mother of Divine Providence. St. Louis-Marie Grignion de Montfort makes this principle the centerpiece of his *Treatise on True Devotion to the Virgin*: "Through the most holy Virgin Mary Jesus Christ came into the world; equally through Her must He reign in the world."[75]

11. "In the End, My Immaculate Heart Will Triumph"

Whatever God wills must come to pass (Judges 9:5); what He does not will will never be carried out in history (Isa. 7:7). Sacred Scripture reiterates this frequently: "I have spoken, I will accomplish it; I have planned it, and I will do it." (Isa. 46:11). The plan of Divine Providence will be infallibly fulfilled, even if we are unaware of its timing and manner. Through all the possible intersections of free wills, humanity is moving toward a historic triumph of Jesus Christ that will precede and prefigure His coming at the end of time. This blessed hour was announced by the Mother of God herself at Fátima with the words, "In the end, my Immaculate Heart will triumph."

---

[75] St. Louis-Marie Grignion de Montfort, *Trattato della vera Devozione*, n. 1.

The triumph announced by our Lady at Fátima confirms the predictions of St. Louis-Marie Grignion de Montfort, who speaks of a "happy time when the divine Mary will be ruler and queen of all hearts,"[76] and through the hearts and minds of men, she will reign in society.

St. Louis-Marie lists the reasons why God wants to reveal and unveil Mary, the masterpiece of His hands, in the historical era that he calls the "century" or "reign" of Mary:

1) Because she hid herself in this world and lowered herself even to dust by her profound humility, having obtained from God that she not be revealed by His disciples and evangelists.

2) Because, being the masterpiece of the hands of God, both here on earth by grace and in Heaven by glory, He wishes to be praised and glorified in her on earth by the living.

3) Just as she is the dawn that precedes and uncovers the Sun of Righteousness that is Jesus Christ, so too she should be known and unveiled so that Jesus Christ may be as well.

76 Ibid., n. 217.

4) Just as she was the route by which Jesus Christ came to us the first time, so will she be when He comes again, albeit not in the same way.

5) Since she is the sure path, the straight and immaculate way to Jesus Christ and to find Him perfectly, it is by her that the souls destined to shine in holiness must find Him. He who finds Mary will find the Life, that is, Jesus Christ, who is the Way, the Truth, and the Life. But he cannot find Mary if he does not seek her; nor can he seek her if he does not know her: for no one seeks or desires what he is unfamiliar with. Therefore, Mary must be known all the more for the greater knowledge and glory of the Most Holy Trinity.

6) Mary must shine more than ever in mercy, strength, and grace, in the last times: in mercy, in order to lead back and receive lovingly the poor sinners and those who have strayed that they may convert and return to the Catholic Church; in strength, against the enemies of God, the idolaters, the schismatics, the Muslims, the Jews, and the hardened impious who will rebel in a terrible way in order to seduce and cause all those who oppose them to fall

with promises and threats. In the end, she must shine in grace to animate and support the brave soldiers and faithful servants of Jesus Christ who will fight for His interests.

7) At last, Mary must be dreadful to the devil and his followers like an army arrayed in battle, especially in these final times, since the devil — knowing well that there is little time remaining for him to lead souls astray — doubles his efforts and attacks each day more than ever. Very soon he will raise cruel persecutions and put grave obstacles in the way of the faithful servants and true children of Mary, against whom he must make greater efforts to overcome them.[77]

The larger framework of the battle is sketched out by the saint under the clear impulse of divine inspiration. Simple souls understand the thought of the saint in its depth, and theologians confirm this prophetic vision.

12. The Reign of Jesus and Mary

The inspired reasons given by St. Louis-Marie can be further expanded upon:

[77] Ibid., n. 50.

1) God, by His free will, desired to choose the most perfect creature, Mary, to crush the rebellion of the ultimate wicked creature, the devil. "What Lucifer lost through pride, Mary gained through humility."[78] To Mary, then, the full and definitive victory over the devil is reserved by Providence.

2) In the image of the Mystical Body of Christ, which is the Church, there is a "*Corpus Mariae*," real and symbolic, constituted by Mary together with her children and her chosen. For St. Louis Grignion de Montfort writes: "All true children of God, and the predestined, have God for their Father and Mary for their Mother."[79] This mystical body is opposed to that "*corpus diaboli*" made up of the devil and his followers, of which St. Augustine,[80] St. Gregory the Great,[81] and many other Church Fathers and theologians speak.[82] There can be no reconciliation for these opposing "families

[78] Ibid.

[79] Ibid., n. 30.

[80] St. Augustine, *De Genesi ad Litteram*, XI, 24, 31; id., *Enarrationes in Ps*, 73, 16; 139, 7.

[81] St. Gregory the Great, *Homelia 16 in Evangelia*; *Moralia*, 4, 14.

[82] St. Ambrose, *In Ps.*, 37, 9; St. Jerome, *In Ezechielem*, 9, 29.

of souls" or "spiritual lineages," only complete enmity, destined to end in the undoing of the children of darkness.

3) The victory of the "Mystical Body" of Mary, united and deployed like an *acies ordinata*, an army arrayed for battle, exalts the Blessed Virgin not only in herself, but in everything that points to her and that comes from her. Thus does she humble her adversary in the most profound manner, destroying all its most poisonous expressions and fruits.

4) Divine Providence has reserved the glory of vanquishing the antichrist and the devil for the Son of God at the end of times, so that He may reign with the Church in eternity. The Son of God has conceded the privilege of defeating the devil in the course of history to His divine Mother so that she may reign with the Church in the luminous era that will precede the reign of the antichrist and the end of the world.

5) The Reign of Mary is nothing less than the triumph of the Church founded by our Lord Jesus Christ as well as the height of Christian civilization, fruit of the merits of His Passion. This historical triumph is necessary so that

> man, with his social nature, may render glory
> to God already in time, the same glory which
> will be rendered to Him by the angels and
> saints in eternity. God is always victorious,
> and His triumph must radiate "on earth as it
> is in Heaven," in time and eternity.

For this reason, St. Louis-Marie speaks of a Second Coming of Jesus upon the earth through Mary, but "glorious and resplendent" as much as the first was secret and hidden: "but both perfect for both will be through Mary."[83] The Reign of Mary will be a poem of glory, just as the Incarnation of the Word was a hidden poem of humility. In this historical era, asserts St. Louis-Marie, the union of Mary with the souls of her apostles will reach an unprecedented intensity and she will shower the graces she has upon the hearts of those faithful to her so abundantly that she will "mold saints so exalted that they will surpass the majority of other saints in their holiness, as much as the cedars of Lebanon surpass shrubs."[84]

Jesus Christ, St. Louis-Marie states, must reign over the world, but "it will be no more than the necessary consequence of the reign of the Most Blessed Virgin Mary, who

---

[83] St. Louis-Marie Grignion de Montfort, *Trattato della vera Devozione*, n. 158.

[84] Ibid., n. 47.

brought Him into the world the first time, and will make Him shine the second."[85]

13. The Reign of Mary and the Reign of the Antichrist

The Reign of Jesus and Mary will be the Reign of the Church and of the Holy Spirit through the closest of bonds that tie the Blessed Virgin to the Mystical Body of Christ, of which she is the heart, as well as to the Third Person of the Most Holy Trinity to whom she is bride. When such an event happens, the work of Divine Providence in history will reach its peak. This will be the brightest spot in history between the Incarnation and the Parousia. The Incarnation opened the historical age of Redemption; the Parousia will bring the end of the history of redeemed humanity. The Reign of Mary will express the communal fulfillment of the fruits of the Redemption. "The Reign of Mary," writes Plinio Corrêa de Oliveira, "is an ordering of things that we understand above all in its temporal aspect, but whose essence lies within the spiritual apex of the Holy Roman Catholic Apostolic Church, through which our Lady reaches the pinnacle of her authority over souls. It will be the greatest moment of glorification in history outside of the Resurrection and Ascension of our Lord Jesus Christ."[86]

[85] Ibid., n. 13.

[86] Cit. in R. de Mattei, Plinio Corrêa de Oliveira, *Profeta del Regno di Maria*, Edizioni Fiducia, Roma 2017, p. 314.

The book of Revelation seems to make reference to this era when it states that the devil will be bound for a thousand years before the coming of the antichrist and the end of the world (Rev. 20:2).

The visions of Revelation remain mysterious. What is certain is that there is no evolutionary process of history: it will conclude with an age of Great Apostasy before Christ seals it with His final victory. Can it be that an hour of darkness in history is possible and an hour of light impossible? Can there be an age in which the darkness of apostasy covers over the world and an age in which it is impossible for light to envelop it? Can there be novelty and progress in evil and yet no novelty or progress in the good? Will God permit days in which the forces of Hell are unleashed with fierce violence and will not all the angels to react with all their power?

This much is clear: we should not expect some future time in which humanity can receive the grace of the Holy Spirit in a different and more perfect manner,[87] but it is allowed, according to St. Thomas, to foresee an age in which the behavior of men changes toward the one and very same law: the movement from public denial of natural and divine law to its public exaltation for the greater glory of God.

---

[87] St. Thomas Aquinas, *Summa Theologiae*, I–II, q. 106, a. 4.

"Mary," writes St. Louis-Marie, "in union with the Holy Spirit produced the greatest thing that there ever was or will be, the Man-God, and as a result will produce the greatest things that will come to pass in the end times."[88]

Over the course of history, men have retreated from God such that they deserved tremendous punishments, as occurred with the water of the flood or the fire which engulfed Sodom and Gomorrah; why then throughout history have these men not drawn closer to God to the point of receiving the spiritual graces that would sanctify an age or a civilization? Would God then allow days of apostasy, but not days of the highest faithfulness to His laws? Would he allow the reign of the antichrist, but not that of His divine Mother?

The era of the antichrist, which will be the darkest hour in history, will be the age of the most fundamental refusal of the natural and divine law. This refusal will be so much more radical and blameworthy because it will oppose the most peaceful and ordered age of history, the era of the Reign of Mary which will precede that of the antichrist and the end times.

[88] St. Louis-Marie Grignion de Montfort, *Trattato della vera Devozione*, n. 35.

14. Parousia, Fulfillment of Divine Plans

The world had a beginning; the world will have an end. There is a final hour in history, a day announced for centuries, an end of times after the Incarnation and the Reign of Mary. This age is the Parousia, the Second Coming of Jesus Christ on earth, the day when the Son of Man will appear in the glory of the Father with His angels to repay to each according to his works (Matt. 16:27, etc.). The return of Christ will take place before the whole world, without any concealment, in the splendor of His glory (Matt. 24:27). The Parousia will signal the end of the world in the complete fulfillment of the end for which it was created (1 Cor. 15:23–28).

The hour of the Parousia is known only to God, although there are some signs noted in Scripture that will precede it: the preaching and acceptance of the Gospel throughout the world (Matt. 24:3–14; Mark 16:15–16; Luke 21:24; Rom. 9:25), the conversion of Israel (Rom. 11:25–27; 2 Cor. 3:14–15), the Great Apostasy (2 Thess. 2:3; Matt. 24:11–12; Luke 17:26–30), the appearance of the antichrist.

"But of that day and hour no one knows, neither the angels of Heaven, nor the Son, but the Father alone" (Matt. 24:36). The fact that we do not know the day or the hour does not mean that we should dismiss from our thoughts the nearness of this moment. The Parousia will be like the *dies natalis*, the birthday, of death; it is an ever-looming sudden reality in which God will come "like a thief" while we sleep "to demand our soul" (Luke 12:20) and to settle the account of our lives. For this reason, the Lord counsels, "Therefore stay awake, for you know neither the day nor the hour."

On that day, trumpets will sound, tombs will open, and the dead will come out resurrected to meet Jesus Christ, who will reveal Himself as King and Judge.[89] The Last Judgment, that is the universal judgment, will be the sovereign act with which He will close the earthly age of the Kingdom of God to usher in His era, glorious and heavenly. The Last Judgment will be the seal that the Man-God will place upon time, the resolution of the mystery of the divine Kingdom (Mark 4:11). The Kingdom of God will appear on earth in all its grandeur. The Judge will be Jesus Christ (John 5:22; Acts 10:42; Rom. 14:10) who will exercise His right as King, Lord, and Redeemer of humanity. He will be surrounded by hosts of angels and saints in a bright halo of clouds of fire, seated in a throne of majesty, assisted in the act of judging by the apostles, martyrs, and those who observed the evangelical counsels. For in that judgment, writes

---

[89] St. Thomas Aquinas, *Contra Gentiles*, IV, 96.

St. Thomas, not only will Christ judge, but all who follow Christ, leaving behind everything, "shall judge nations" (Wisd. 3:8).[90]

God and the world, Creator and creatures, Mary with her children, the devil with his followers: all will be gathered together, facing one another. All angels and all men will be judged on their thoughts, words, acts, and omissions. The judgment, notes Fr. Schmaus, will not be pronounced only upon individuals, but also upon peoples, because the entirety of history is approach toward or retreat from God by peoples.[91] For peoples, as such, do not survive solely to the end of history, because there is no Heaven nor Hell for them, but they will survive into eternity, honored or dishonored, in the men who make them up, because they will carry the sign of their affiliation to their nations and their families. That is why, in Revelation, it reads: "every eye will see him, even those who pierced him. All the peoples of the earth will lament him" (Rev. 1:7; John 19:37). The supreme judgment will consider all the events of history, moment by moment, at every point in space, not only horizontally across time which runs through today and tomorrow, but also and especially the vertical line that connects them to the singular

---

[90] Id., *Compendium Theologiae*, II, cap. 245, nn. 540–542.

[91] M. Schmaus, *Dogmatica cattolica*, cit., vol. IV, 1, p. 244.

moment of eternity.[92] The sentence will be given by a collective internal enlightenment by which all intelligent beings will know their own actions and those of others in their individual value and in their communal repercussions with regard to the whole of history. The extent of nations', peoples', and civilizations' conformity to grace will be revealed; the significance of heresies, wars, and revolutions will be clear; and the actions of men in their social and political dimensions will be made known.

15. The Revelation of Divine Providence

The Last Judgment will finally reveal the mysterious and wondrous designs of Divine Providence. "There is nothing concealed that will not be revealed, nor secret that will not be known" (Luke 12:2). The general disclosure of consciences will be so clear that no one will be unaware of anything, whether regarding his own conscience or that of others. "The most hidden wounds of our heart will be illuminated before Him who is the light of the world."[93] All meaning throughout history, all the mysteries and perplexities of the world will be unraveled before the universal

---

[92] Mons. Antonio Piolanti, *Giudizio*, in *Enciclopedia Cattolica*, vol. VI, p. 732.

[93] Louis Lallemant, *Dottrina spirituale*, tr. Ital. Paoline, Roma 1985, p. 318.

assembly. The Last Judgment will be history unveiled and re-vealed. "Then," writes St. Ephrem, the great bard of the Parousia, "the Lord will appear in Heaven like lightning in indescribable glory. The angels and archangels will march before His glory like flames of fire and like a seething river. The Cherubim will bow their heads and the Seraphim will fly, crying out in terror: 'Awaken, you who are asleep, behold the Bridegroom who comes.' Then the tombs will be opened wide and in the blink of an eye all peoples will rise and see the holy beauty of the Bridegroom."[94]

Jesus Christ will be exalted before the whole world as King and Judge upon the throne of glory. St. Michael the Archangel and all the angels will cast Satan and his followers into a "pool of fire" (Rev. 20:10). The public and universal condemnation of every sin with all of its consequences will restore the external glory taken away from God, while the triumph of Jesus Christ and all the members of His Mystical Body will be the ultimate reward of the just. "Everything will come to an end with the sentence that the supreme Judge will audibly pass with His most sacred human lips."[95] After this irrevocable sentence, adds Fr. Lallemant, "all

---

[94] St. Ephrem, Sec. Adv., VII, 11, in *Assemani*, II, 230, cit. in Jean Daniélou, *Gli Angeli e la loro missione*, Edizioni Paoline, Pescara 1957, p. 132.

[95] L. Lallemant, *Dottrina spirituale*, cit., p. 318

creatures, allying themselves with God, will arm themselves for the execution of His retribution and when every plan is fulfilled, the course of the ages will come to an end and time will disappear into the bosom of eternity."[96] The temporal reign of Christ will give way to His eternal kingdom.

The Man-God will present the Church, His bride, in the fullness of the divine Glory to the Father and the whole world. He will introduce her into the glory of His Kingdom where she will appear immaculate and radiant as she was conceived by God from eternity.

The world will not be destroyed but rather transformed into a new Heaven and a new earth (Rev. 21:1). This renewed creation will express the glory of God in the highest form accorded to creatures by God. On that luminous day without evening, glorified man will be able to fix his eyes effortlessly upon the hidden treasures of creation and contemplate — no longer through reflections or in riddles — their wonders. "One would have to ask Eastern poetry for all the enchantment of its Heaven, all the charm of its inflamed imagination, all the impetus of its creative genius, in order to reach only a shadow of that marvelous picture that will be laid out for the contemplation of the glorified man. One would need to ask

96   Ibid.

the faith for all the splendors of revelation to be able to imagine in any semblance the sublime spectacle of a nature that will be entirely renewed as soon as the King of life and glory sends you His life-giving spirit (Ps. 104:30)."[97]

A song of praise will rise from the world, which will at last radiate all the divine splendor as though in a mirror of perfect reflections. Jesus Christ will liberate the visible world from every evil and every disorder, and He will fill it with His glory just as the life-giving sun fills the world with its light. A great fire of love will blaze throughout creation, burning men and matter without consuming them, but illuminating them with an inextinguishable splendor.

The last day of the world will be a poem of boundless triumph. The promises of the Old and New Testament will finally be fulfilled. Creation will render all the splendor of its glory to God. What He had willed in the beginning will in the end be just as He had determined. Divine Providence will celebrate its dazzling and ultimate triumph over chaos, sin, and revolution.

---

[97] N. Taccone-Gallucci, *L'uomo-Dio*, cit., vol. II, pp. 246–47.

PART TWO

The Sacred Order of
the Universe

1. Divine Providence Is the First Principle of Created Things

Divine Providence is God Himself, considered in one of His infinite perfections.

God, incomprehensible in His essence, is without parts or divisions, without limits or horizons, unchangeable and eternal, immense and omnipresent, infinitely rich in perfection and infinitely simple in His single perfection. The divine perfections, many-faceted and different to the eyes of man, constitute a single and most simple perfection in God, just as the innumerous drops of the sea form one single waveless ocean that encompasses them all. Of these perfections, the first is Being, a quality God Himself revealed to Moses in the burning bush: "I am who I am ... This is what you will tell the Israelites: I AM has sent me to you" (Exod. 3:14). All divine attributes spring forth from Being as from a primordial fount.

The first aspect of Being is unity, or rather it is to be a beginning — or principle.[98] All created things, however, in order to be, must have a first principle that constitutes them, while God has no need of created things to be a beginning. God is the first, the only, and the absolute principle, because He has the totality and fullness of being. The divine essence is nothing other than His being.[99] God is that which He is or, more simply, He IS.

In His aspect of first principle of created things, God may be defined as Divine Providence. Indeed, Providence encapsulates all of the relations the universe has with God, which are reduced to how an effect relates to a cause or, in a wider sense, of how order relates to a first principle. In this sense, Providence expresses the sovereignty, perfectly just and infinitely merciful, of God over all creation.

"With the name *God*," says St. Bonaventure, "the first and highest principle of all things is meant."[100] For this reason, first principle of all creatures and of each creature in particular is found among the names of God: "God," writes the great theologian Lessius, "is called the first principle of

---

[98]   St. Thomas Aquinas, *De Veritate*, q. 1, a. 1; *Summa Theologiae*, I, q. 13, a. 11.

[99]   Id., *Compendium Theologiae*, I, cap. 11, n. 20; *De Ente et Essentia*, V.

[100]   St. Bonaventure, *Quaestiones Disputatae de Mysterio Trinitatis*, q. 2, a. 1, concl. t. V.

all creatures and of each in particular, because every creature, in whatever degree it depends on multiple causes, like plants, animals, works of art, has its final end in God alone, as the first of all causes."[101]

God is the first cause and the first principle of all that exists, "origin of all things and their final fulfillment."[102] He is the principle that depends upon nothing, from which all derives, to which all returns: "[He is] the Alpha and the Omega, the first and the last, the beginning and the end," as the book of Revelation reveals to us (22:13). Dom François de Sales Pollien comments: "All is made by God; all is made for Him. Nothing exists without Him; nothing exists if not for Him. All comes from Him; all goes to Him. He is the only beginning and the ultimate end. Only He is the beginning, only He is the end."[103]

Divine Providence is the manifestation of the glory of God in the created universe.

2. The Triple Causality of the Universe

The name of first principle expresses the relationship that runs between God and the universe in terms of cause and

---

[101] Léonarde Lessius S.J., *Les noms divins*, Gauthiers-Villars, Paris 1884, p. 103.

[102] St. Bonaventure, *Breviloquium*, part I, ch. V, n. 8.

[103] Dom François de Sales Pollien, *La vita interiore semplificata e ricondotta al suo fondamento*, tr. Ital. Paoline, Roma 1969, p. 54.

effect. This causal relationship can be considered in three ways. When we assert that everything is made by God and that God is the origin of all things, we express the efficient causality of the first principle; when we say that God is the fulfillment of all things, the common good toward which everything tends and to which all returns, we make clear its final causality. But the creation and preservation of creatures according to a plan is also an act particularly of God, and in this we can see the exemplary causality of the first principle.[104] It is in fact a law of creation that everything that exists not only has a beginning and tends toward an end, but also that it moves in the universe reflecting an exemplar.

The efficient cause is that which begets action; the final cause is that toward which an action tends; the exemplar cause is that which an action models itself after in its movement. The principle of final causality moves down, so to speak, from the efficient cause to its ultimate effect, while the principle of efficient causality rises from the result of the action to that cause which produces it. The exemplar cause unites, in a certain respect, the efficient causality and the final causality in the perfection of a type or ideal model which the action resembles. This brings forth a necessary degree of

---

[104] St. Thomas Aquinas, *Summa Theologiae*, I, q. 44, a. 3.

beauty and splendor. The efficient cause is associated with the attribute of truth, the final cause with that of goodness, and the exemplar cause with that of beauty.

In this triple causality of the one principle, the divine Trinity is manifested. The first principle of the universe, which is at once efficient cause, exemplar cause, and final cause of all creation, indeed corresponds to the Most Holy Trinity, a single God in three distinct persons. According to this trinitarian relationship of causality, "each creature," says St. Bonaventure, "is constituted into being from the efficient cause, conforms itself to the exemplar cause, and is ordered toward the end."[105] The Seraphic Doctor sees in the Father the efficient cause of all things, in the Son the exemplar cause through which things have form and beauty, in the Holy Spirit their final cause. To the Father, the Son, and the Holy Spirit are due Power, Wisdom, and Goodness respectively, the three attributes with which the Most Holy Trinity is praised within Holy Scripture.[106] Leo XIII recalls: "Very appropriately has the Church consistently attributed to the Father works of Power, to the Son those of Wisdom, and to the Spirit those of Love."[107]

---

[105] St. Bonaventure, *Breviloquium*, part II, ch. I, n. 4.

[106] Ibid, part I, ch. VI, n. 5.

[107] Leo XIII, Encyclical *Divinum Illud Munus*, May 9, 1897.

With Wisdom, God knows and orders that which He wishes to do; with Goodness, He loves and wills it; with Power, He accomplishes it. That which the Lord arranges and wills, He can do, and He can do everything, for He can will and order everything: "*Ipse est omnipotens super omnia opera sua*" (Sir. 43:20). Wisdom, Goodness, and Power form in God an absolute unity: these three perfections are the constituents of Divine Providence, which possesses them in a single and simultaneous act of being.[108]

3. The Three Perfections of Divine Providence

St. Thomas defines Providence as "the ordering of things toward their end,"[109] in terms analogous to those by which St. Augustine defines order: "that by which all things that God has made are governed."[110] In a wider sense, we can define Divine Providence as the perfection of order conceived in eternity by the Divine Wisdom and actualized in time by the omnipotent will of God, or rather, figuratively speaking, as the hand of God, which carries out in time that which the Divine Mind has thought and willed from eternity. Providence is therefore the unfolding of a divine plan within

---

[108] St. Thomas Aquinas, *De Veritate*, q. 5, a. 1.

[109] Id., *Summa Theologiae*, I, q. 22, a. 5.

[110] St. Augustine, *De Ordine*, I, 10, 28.

created time and space. St. Dionysius defines divinity as "Providence which watches over all and which in full goodness both observes and embraces everything, filling with itself, and surpassing all things which benefit from its Providence."[111] This plan is immense and eternal, because it acts in every place and every moment of the universe. In fact, God "embraces the totality of that which was, of that which is, and of that which will be in a single act that does not begin ever again."[112]

We may also say that Divine Providence is the order of the universe considered in the triple expression of its singular principle: the efficient causality, the final causality, and the exemplar causality. Providence is the final cause of all created things because it orders them to the ultimate end of the universe, which is the Divine Good; it is the efficient cause of the universe, because it creates from nothing and keeps it in being with its omnipotence; it is furthermore the exemplar cause because in all things created and sustained in being it imprints order and the reflection of the Divine Wisdom. The vastness of the universe, according to Hugh of Saint Victor, manifests the

---

[111] Dionysius the Areopagite, *De Divinis Nominibus*, XII, 2.

[112] Marie-Joseph Nicolas O.P., *Provvidenza*, tr. Ital. San Paolo, Cinisello Balsamo 1999, p. 8.

power of God, the usefulness of all that exists expresses His goodness; its beauty reveals His wisdom. Of these three divine attributes, the first to make itself clear to the contemplation of man is beauty.[113]

The priest Luis de la Puente sees these three perfections symbolized by the three fingers with which God holds up the earth, according the words of the prophet Isaiah: "*Appendit tribus digitis molem terrae*" (Isa. 4:12).[114] Divine Providence is the Most Holy Trinity considered in His relationship with created things that it preserves in being, loves, and directs to their end.

When St. Paul says "from him and through him and for him are all things" (Rom. 11:36), he shows the Father as the highest original principle from which every action proceeds, the Son as the Wisdom of God through whom the Father acts, and the Holy Spirit as the final end of every divine activity.

It is a dogma of faith: "God, with His Providence, protects and governs all that He has created, because 'Indeed, she spans the world from end to end mightily and governs all things well' (Wisd. 8:1)."

---

[113] Hugh of Saint Victor, *Didascalicon,* in P.L., 175, vol. VII, 823–24.

[114] Venerable Luis de la Puente, *Meditazioni,* tr. Ital. Marietti, Torino-Roma 1927, vol. VI, p. 245.

4. The Divine Power as Efficient Causality of the Universe

The infinite power of the Most Holy Trinity expresses itself above all in the act of creation. "You created all things; because of your will they came to be and were created" (Rev. 4:11). Nothing was outside of God before the creation of the world: there was only God, and all things, visible and invisible, received the being that they have from Him.[115] He had no need of any preexisting material in order to create: He made everything from nothing, giving to those things their being: "*Ipse dixit, et facta sunt: ipse mandavit, et creata sunt*" (Ps. 32:9). He spoke, and all things were made; he commanded, and all things were created.

To create is to bring something from nothing into being, without any previous material with which to make use of.[116] But between nothing and being there is an immeasurable gap that only an infinite cause can overcome. The existence even of a single atom in the universe would suffice to demonstrate the existence of God and of His infinite power. For the importance of the creative act does not lie in producing a particle of the smallest order or in making the immeasurable vastness of

---

[115] Lateran Council IV, Ch. I, *De Fide Catholica*, in Denz-H, n. 800.

[116] St. Thomas Aquinas, II Sent., d. 1, p. 1, a. 2, q. 2; *Summa Theologiae*, I, q. 46, a. 1–2; *Compendium Theologiae*, I, ch. 69.

the universe in its entirety, but rather in the creation of something from nothing, no matter its size and scope.

The relation between God and creature does not dissipate at the moment of its creation, but it continues in every single moment of its existence. One divine act has produced each and every thing's being, and it preserves it in every moment of time. By their creation, things arise from nothing; by their preservation, they persist in being.

With the same act by which He creates, God preserves His creatures.[117] The act of creation, so removed in time, is miraculously renewed each day. If God should pause this continual action which keeps things in their being, the movements of the Heavens and the light of the universe would cease, things would dissolve and fall back into the abyss of nothingness. Hence the words of Scripture: "[God] sustains all things by his mighty word" (Heb. 1:3).

In the relentless flow of time, all that exists lives thanks to this creative act which keeps it afloat above the abyss of nothingness. That which is created thereby participates in the divine being and can be defined as a "being by participation," in the words of St. Thomas, because it has being, but it is not the Being which it receives.[118]

---

[117] Id., *De Potentia*, 5, 1, ad 2.
[118] Id., *Summa Theologiae*, I, q. 3, a. 4.

To participate means to receive. Created things have their own essence, distinct from the being that they receive. They are composed, in short, of being and of essence: their being which they participate in, from God, and the essence which specifies their mode of being in creation. Being does not belong to created things, while essence is their specific perfection, that by which we can talk about something as being what it is.[119] For this reason the Angelic Doctor affirms that "Just as each creature receives its being from another and is considered in itself nothing, it must be sustained by something else in order to be preserved, it can fall into nothingness on its own, if God should not sustain it."[120]

5. The Divine Goodness as Final Causality of the Universe

The highest good, says St. Augustine, is called the "end" because it is for this end that we want all other things and this end we want for itself.[121] All that God has made has been created for an end. This end, St. Thomas confirms, is nothing other than the Goodness itself of God.[122] God

---

[119] Id., *De Ente et Essentia*, I, 5.

[120] Id., *Summa Theologiae*, I–IIae, q. 109, a. 2, ad 2.

[121] St. Augustine, *De Civitate Dei*, VIII, n. 8.

[122] St. Thomas Aquinas, *Compendium Theologiae*, I, ch. 101, n. 194.

creates for Himself, for His goodness and the glorification of His goodness is the primary end of creation.

God, most perfect Being, could not add some good or perfection to Himself with His creation. The divine Being did not create in order to attain some good, but rather in order to pour out and communicate His goodness. The good that He communicated to the universe, by creating it, was none other than Himself, supreme Good to which all creatures tend, for they originate from Him.

God can have neither cause nor end external to His infinite being: for nothing is outside of Him. He acts, as pure Act, but does not tend in His action toward something that He does not have, because He lacks nothing. For this reason, while all creatures act based upon the desire of an end, God instead acts out of love for what He Himself possesses, since nothing can be added to His perfection. Therefore, the end of creation is not the participation of goodness in the universe, but the Divine Goodness itself, which God wishes to communicate. "For He acts through His goodness not as if searching for that which He does not have, but wishing to communicate that which He has."[123] *Deus caritas est* (1 John 4:16).

---

[123] Id., *De Potentia*, q. 3, a. 15, ad 14.

God has created out of love, and love for the objective goodness of His Being is the primary end of creation.

The secondary end is the good and the perfection of the creatures themselves, especially rational creatures.[124] Goodness, insofar as it is communicated and poured out, is the end of God who creates, while inasmuch as it is participated in, it is the end of the creatures who by loving God render glory unto Him. For this reason, that canticle of glory to God rises from creation, which St. Francis so wonderfully summed up: "Highest, all-powerful, and good Lord … Yours are the praises and every blessing … may You be praised, my Lord … by all Your creatures."

The glory of God is the end of creation. It cannot search for another end and another good in the universe apart from this.

"The Lord has made everything for His glory" (see Prov. 16:4). The manifestation and the glorification of the goodness of God is the first end of creation because the only good of God and of the universe is His glory. For this, "The Heavens declare the glory of God" (Ps. 19:2) and the angels announce "glory to God in the highest," which corresponds to,

---

[124] Msgr. Antonio Piolanti, *Dio nel mondo e nell'uomo*, Desclée, Roma 1959, pp. 78–88.

as its reflection, the "[peace] on earth ... to those on whom his favor rests" (Luke 2:14).

All creation reflects the glory of God. Dante carved this into his verses: "The glory of Him who moves all / radiates through the universe and shimmers / in one part more and less elsewhere."[125]

6. The Divine Wisdom as Exemplar Causality of the Universe

All that is created and sustained in being by the Divine Power does not only tend toward the Goodness of God and His glory, but it also bears some resemblance to God, first principle of the universe and its exemplar cause, in His own attribute of Divine Wisdom. From Wisdom, "the reflection of eternal light, the spotless mirror of the power of God, the image of his goodness," comes the order and beauty of the universe (Wisd. 7:25–26).

Wisdom is the perfect image of God, who with a single eternal act knows His entire divine being, and expresses all that He knows in a single eternal word: The Word, the second Person of the Most Holy Trinity.

[125] Dante Alighieri, *Paradiso*, 1, ll, 1–3.

The second Person of the Most Holy Trinity, Wisdom substantial and uncreated, is defined as eternal Wisdom, if considered in His eternal begetting, or Wisdom incarnate, which is Jesus Christ Himself, if understood in space and time.

For this reason, Sacred Scripture attributes the creation and rule of all things to Wisdom, which is the prudent rule of God. Indeed, it is written in Proverbs (3:19–20): "The Lord by wisdom founded the earth, established the Heavens by prudence; By his wisdom the depths are split, and the clouds drop down dew." The Wisdom of God, it is said, "spans the world from end to end mightily and governs all things well" (Wisd. 8:1).

Wisdom says of itself, in the books of Solomon: "*Ab aeterno* I was formed, at the first, before the earth. When there were no deeps I was brought forth" (Prov. 8:23–24). Eternal Wisdom began to shine out from the bosom of God when He made light, Heaven, and earth. She separated, formed, measured, and weighed; she, writes St. Louis-Marie Grignion de Montfort, gave order to the Heavens and the earth, designed the firmament, fixed the places of the planets, laid the foundations of the earth; she defined the diversity and variety of the angels, men, and of every created thing, and established the mysterious law of nature and of the universe.[126]

---

[126] St. Louis-Marie Grignion de Montfort, *L'Amour de la Sagesse Eternelle*, nn. 35–36.

Divine Providence is — first and foremost — order and it is a characteristic of Wisdom to order.[127] She arranges "all things by measure and number and weight" (Wisd. 11:20). "Weight," says St. Bonaventure, "which makes things tend toward a determined position; number, which distinguishes them from one another; measure, by which they are delimited."[128] Number, weight, and measure are the conditions of every finite and loved being: from these three derive the multiplicity of things and the variety of their beauty.[129] The beauty of the universe is in the multiplicity of its parts, but also in their unity, for the diversity of things is beautiful, but so too are the things within them that remain the same and do not change. Proportion is the beauty of the material multiplicity of the universe, its radiance is the beauty of its spiritual unity.

In this infinitely harmonious light, as Donoso Cortés observes, all created things continue to be in the divine intellect, as they were before their creation, in accordance with a model that is in Him from time eternal: "All things are found there for that highest reason that wills effects to be

---

[127] St. Thomas Aquinas, *De Trinitate*, II, 2, 1; *Summa Theologiae*, I–IIae, q. 57, a. 2; *Summa Contra Gentiles*, II, 24.

[128] St. Bonaventure, *Itinerarium Mentis in Deum*, I, n. 11.

[129] Id., *I Sent.* 43, art. 3, concl.

subordinate to causes, consequences subordinate to principles, reflections subordinate to light, and forms subordinate to their archetypes. In Him the vastness of the sea, the lushness of the fields, the harmony of the heavenly bodies, the perfection of worlds, the brilliance of the stars, the magnificence of the firmament are all encompassed. In Him is the measure, the weight, and the number of everything; and all things had their origin in number, weight, and measure. The highest, inviolable laws of all beings are in God, and each of these laws is subject to His rule. All that has life has its causes in Him; trees find in Him the laws of vegetation, every moving thing finds in Him the laws of movement, all that has sensation finds in Him the laws of feeling, everything that has intelligence finds in Him the laws of understanding, all that has freedom finds in Him the laws of the will. Therefore, it may be asserted without fear of falling into pantheism that all things are in God and God is in all things."[130]

7. The Ladder of Beings and of Perfections

"In the beginning, God created the Heavens and the earth" (Gen. 1:1). With this striking truth, Sacred Scripture and the story of the universe is opened. Heaven and earth and all

---

[130] Juan Donoso Cortés, *Saggio sul cattolicesimo, il liberalismo e il socialismo*, tr. Ital. Rusconi Editore, Milano 1972, pp. 47–48.

things visible and invisible have their beginning. With analogous words, St. John begins his Gospel: "In the beginning was the Word, and the Word was with God, and the Word was God. He was in the beginning with God. All things came to be through him, and without him nothing came to be" (John 1:1–3).

An endless ladder of beings and perfections wonderfully unfolds in the time and space created by the *fiat* of the Divine Light. The created light, which this very instant gives the universe its variety, is the symbol and expression of the Light of being which distinguishes things in the unity of their principle. "Among all the corporeal things," writes St. Bonaventure, "the light is that which can most be assimilated into the eternal Light."[131]

God is the cause of being for all that there is, insofar as He conveys being to all things, just as the sun conveys light to the air and to the other beings which are illuminated by it.[132] Light, which radiates through all things, is the most active and most noble substance of the visible universe and the source of the perfection of corporeal things. In view of this, the earth is lower and darker, while Heaven is higher

---

[131] St. Bonaventure, *II Sentent.*, 13, a 2, 2, 83.

[132] St. Thomas Aquinas, *Compendium Theologiae*, I, ch. 6–8, n. 117; ch. 130, n. 261.

and nobler. Heaven, then, in its splendor, constitutes the transition, as it were, between the perceptible world and the spiritual world. Between earth and Heaven, the ladder of created beings is defined by the participation in being and the Divine Light, of which material light is both a symbol and reflection.

On earth, this great ladder of created beings extends from inorganic matter through to man. From arid sands and the smallest living microorganisms through to mankind and the angels, every creature has its own tier of perfection. And each tier, according to its ascending intensity, brings its creature to the ultimate good, the transcendent and uncreated Creator of the universe.

The ladder of beings and perfections is not comprised solely of creatures in a strict sense, such as the angels, mankind, and the animals. It also includes all that is created by these beings or that which influences them. This is the miraculous show that the universe presents in the constant and perpetual motion of its forces; the transformation of the elements that make up matter, the intelligible word of man, the flash of thought, the fire of love — all springs forth from the being of things.[133]

[133] Nicola Taccone Gallucci, *L'Uomo-Dio*, Lodovico Felice Cagliati, Milano 1881 (reprint 1997), vol. II, pp. 149–50.

In this ladder, in which all things are ordered to Divine Goodness, each molecule of the universe acts on all others and is affected by all others. "That which science calls 'the force of attraction,'" writes Ernest Hello, "should be called the 'law of attraction.' For forces are not laws imposed upon nature by a higher will."[134]

This ladder of perfections and created beings is not familiar with "evolution," but only harmony and order. If the ladder of living species were the result of an evolutionary movement and therefore a perfecting movement of nature, the history of the universe should record, in the passing of time, a great number of imperfect species. In truth, it is precisely the opposite. A blade of grass is no less perfect than a cedar of Lebanon; a ladybug is no less perfect than a person.[135]

God could have made a world different from our own and, had He wished, a more perfect one. But He could not have better conceived that world that He freely wished to create. "All creatures of the perceptible world direct the soul that can see and reason to God eternal. In fact, all are shadows,

---

[134] Ernest Hello, *L'uomo* [L'Homme], tr. Ital. Carabba, Lanciano 1912, p. 49.

[135] Mons. Pier Carlo Landucci, *Il Dio in Cui Crediamo*, Edizioni Pro Sanctitate, Roma 1968, p. 96.

echoes, and representations; they are impressions and simulacra of that first principle which is the highest Power, Wisdom, and Goodness, that Light that creates and fills everything, that Artful and Ordering Mind, which is the efficient and exemplar cause of everything. All things are formed as though one great mirror that is placed before our eyes so that we may contemplate God."[136]

8. God and the Material World

The glory of God is nothing but the representation of His splendor in creation, or rather the beauty of His perfections, reflected as in a mirror. God, observes Hugh of Saint Victor, did not only wish that the world should exist, but that it should be beautiful and wonderful.[137] Creation reflects the beauty of God because it bears some likeness to Him. Likeness, which does not imply equality but rather differentiation, is the sole relationship that can be established between an effect and the cause that produces and transcends it. God thereby created a universe distinct from Him, one that by participating in His goodness and His perfection represents Him without being the highest good and infinite perfection,

---

[136] St. Bonaventure, *Itinerarium Mentis in Deum*, cap. II, n. 11.
[137] Hugh of St. Victor, *De Arrha Animae*, 960–61.

i.e., without being another God, for that would be paradoxical and absurd.[138]

Differentiation characterizes not only the relationship between the universe and God, but also the relationship between created things themselves, for the array of creatures represents the divine perfection with a greater richness than one limited creature.[139] For this reason, St. Thomas Aquinas affirms that "the ultimate perfection of the universe is the diversity of things."[140] Good and the perfection of everything results from the reciprocal order of the parts.[141]

In contrast to the perfect and absolute unity of God, there is a metaphysical and innumerable unity, as the Angelic Doctor explains, in the diversity and multiplicity of creation. Every creature is one and identical to itself, as it has its own essence and nature which defines it, yet it is varied because it is distinct from the other creatures. From the mathematical perspective, the principle that reduces different entities into a single relationship is its ratio. From the metaphysical perspective, it is its participation. All creatures have a single cause in Being and a

138 St. Thomas Aquinas, *De Veritate*, q. 2, 21; *Contra Gentiles*, II, 25.

139 Id., *Contra Gentiles*, II, 45; *Summa Theologiae*, I, q. 47, aa. 1 e 2.

140 Id., *Summa Theologiae*, I, q. 47, a. 1.

141 Ibid., I, q. 61, aa. 3 e 4.

different participation in Being and the Good which distinguishes them.

The universe presents itself as an order that defers to a principle which transcends it, and which derives its ultimate meaning from it.[142] In this harmonious order lies the beauty of the universe whose symbol is the starry sky.

The ladder of degrees of perfection is measured by the relative resemblance or unlikeness with regard to the absolute and original divine perfection. God, most perfect Being itself, is the principle that measures the ladder, ascending or descending, depending on whether one approaches Him or distances oneself from Him. But this ladder does not include God at the summit. God is beyond the order of creation and its degrees of perfection because He is its transcendent and supreme model and cause.

In this ascent toward God, all creation expresses the divine glory, each individual part in its own way and at its own level. The higher beings do so spiritually, while the lower beings do so materially, "so that all the different grades of goodness maybe realized."[143] For St. Thomas explains that, in a sense, two poles exist in relation to which things are ordered: God and matter. That which is closer to

[142] Ibid., I, q. 49.
[143] Ibid., I, q. 48, a. 2.

matter is less perfect in itself, but that which is closer to God expresses a higher grade of perfection.[144]

The reality of matter does not reduce to the experiential, but consists in something more intimate, undetectable, which is found beyond appearances. Modern science speaks of molecules, formed by a network of atoms, themselves composed of other infinitesimally small particles, which continue to be given new names. In reality, it is not possible to give a purely physical explanation for the atomic and subatomic particles that make up matter, disregarding their metaphysical properties.

In reality, the ladder of beings is characterized by a principle that distinguishes them and isolates them in their unrepeatability: their form. There is no first matter in and of itself, without a form that defines it, or rather without a principle that determines its essence and structure. Everything is made from matter and form. Form is the principle which gives being and life to things.

9. Man, Summit of Visible Creation

God communicated being and goodness to creatures according to various grades of beauty and perfection. To some He gave only corporeal being, like the Heavens and the earth; to others

[144] Id., *De Substantiis Separatis*, ch. 6, n. 39.

He gave vegetative life, like the trees, flowers, and plants; to others still He gave sensate life, like the animals, birds, and fishes; to a last group, He gave spiritual being, like the angels.

On the sixth day, God created man, in His image and likeness (Gen. 1:26); with him, the last of all things created, God finished His work of creation. The Lord formed man from mud of the earth, into which He breathed the breath of life, and man became a living person (Gen. 2:7). To him He gave a piece of every creature. Of this St. Gregory says that man has "being in common with the rocks, life in common with the trees, senses in common with the animals, and understanding in common with the angels."[145] Through the soul, man has that for which he is man: ensouled, living, body, substance, and being. "Therefore, the soul imparts to man every essential degree of perfection, and moreover communicates to the body the act of being, through which it itself is."[146] To man, made of body and soul, God gave dominion and use of all creatures of the earth, a dominion which He left him, in part, even after his sin. "Let us make human beings in our image, after our likeness. Let them

---

[145] St. Gregory the Great, *XL Homiliarum in Evangelia*, Lib. II, Homilia XXIX, 1570.

[146] *Decree of the Congregatio studiorum*, July 27, 1914, in Denz-H, n. 3616.

have dominion over the fish of the sea, the birds of the air, the tame animals, all the wild animals, and all the creatures that crawl on the earth. God created mankind in his image" (Gen. 1:26–27). Man was placed by God as the head and crown of creation, to whom all should be ordered so that he might order all to God as the representative of the cosmos.

"For we see," writes St. Thomas, "that certain realities of the lowest order participate in the divine likeness only as to their being, such as the inanimate realities; others, rather, do so as to both being and living, such as plants; others still as to understanding, such as animals; but the supreme act of understanding is that which is had with the intellect, and this is — to the highest degree — proper to God. The supreme creatures are therefore those of the intellect; and since these among all creatures are those who most closely approach resemblance with God, for this reason they are created in the image of God."[147]

The Angelic Doctor further writes that in a particular way, the perfection of the entire embodied nature of the universe depends on the perfection of man.[148] The perfection of man consists in his achievement of his ultimate end, which is perfect blessedness, or namely happiness. This

[147] St. Thomas Aquinas, *Compendium Theologiae*, I, ch. 75, n. 132.
[148] Ibid., I, ch. 149, n. 297.

consists in the vision of God. Therefore, the final end of the intellectual creature is to know God in His essence.[149]

"The masterpiece of visible creation, image of God," observes Dom Pollien, "man is the final and highest link in the chain of earthly beings, in him the creative work ends. Having a material body and spiritual soul, he participates in both the visible and invisible world. By carrying in his body a likeness to the lower beings, and in his soul the very resemblance to God, he is placed between creature and God as a link between matter and spirit, like the link between earth and Heaven."[150]

10. The Freedom of the Rational Creature

In man, composed both of soul and body, the higher part is the soul, by its nature both incorruptible and immortal. The beauty of man is first of all the beauty of the soul and of its faculties. The soul is the mirror of divine perfection, but it does not spring forth from divine substance, like the Gnostics contended, for God makes it directly *ex nihilo*.[151] The soul is the vital principle of the body and informs it in its entirety, without residing in any part of it. Its principle faculties are

[149] Ibid., I, ch. 104, I, q. 12, a. 1.

[150] Dom F. Pollien, *La Vita Interiore Semplificata*, cit., p. 56.

[151] Denz-H, nn. 190, 201, 285, 455, 685.

reason, through which man understands truth, and the will, by which he loves the good.

Although the intellect precedes the will because it enlightens it and enables it to turn toward the good, the will is the decisive faculty in man.[152] The will freely chooses the supreme good from those presented to it as good by the intellect and loves it. St. Francis de Sales asserts, "the will does not recognize the good except by means of the intellect, but once it has discovered it, it no longer needs the intellect to exercise its love."[153] So too, observes Fr. García de Haro, "The will that seeks God also contains the highest love of neighbor and of the world."[154] Therefore, in the human soul, the highest and noblest thing that exists is the free will that unites itself to God through its love. For God is love (1 John 4:8), and the specific act of the will is love, that is, the intimate and affectionate union with the known good. The Angelic Doctor affirms that "Love of God is greater than knowing him."[155]

---

[152] Adolphe Tanquerey, *Compendio di ascetica e mistica*, tr. Ital. Desclée de Brouwer, Roma 1928, p. 509.

[153] St. Francis de Sales, *Trattato dell'Amor di Dio*, tr. Ital. Paoline, Milano 1989, p. 442.

[154] Ramon García de Haro, *La vita cristiana*, Ares, Milano 1995, p. 177.

[155] St. Thomas Aquinas, *Summa Theologiae*, I, q. 82, a. 3; II–IIae, q. 23, a. 6 ad 1.

Indeed, the one who understands the good is not good, but the one who loves it is, just as he who understands evil is not evil, but he who desires it is. "Similarly, it is worse to hate God than not to know him or not to think of Him."[156]

Man is the image of God because, unlike irrational beings, he is the master of his own acts. What defines his freedom is the power to direct his own acts to their end: it is an active movement that makes man the "principle of his own acts as God is."[157] Thanks to the gift of freedom, man is the source of his own acts and participates in the divine causality. He can direct himself to the good that he knows.

Freedom is not the possibility to choose between good and bad, but rather the capacity of the will to accomplish the good. In a more profound sense, freedom can be defined as will ordered to the good. The will which chooses the bad is not free, but a slave, because "everyone who commits sin is a slave of sin" (John 8:34, Rom. 6:20). As St. Thomas notes, "In this sense, the blessed and the angels, who cannot sin, are freer than us."[158] The greatest slavery is that which comes from the devil, who in renouncing the divine good has irrevocably refused to be

---

[156] Blessed John Duns Scotus, *Opus Oxoniense*, IV, d. 49, n. 10.

[157] St. Thomas Aquinas, *Summa Theologiae*, I–IIae, Prolog.

[158] Id., *Summa Theologiae*, I, q. 62, a. 8, ad 3.

free. He hates God and serves Him against his will. *In statu termini*, that is, in the final state, the angels and men are immutably fixed in their conscience and love of the Absolute; *in statu viae*, or in the state of journeying, the angels and men know the Absolute, not in the clarity of vision, but only in the night of faith.[159] One must choose for or against him because " 'No one can serve two masters.' ... You cannot serve God and mammon" (Matt. 6:24).

Freedom then is the capacity of the rational creature to move itself of its own accord toward its proper end; the capacity given to man to govern himself and to join himself to God is his singular good.[160] That is why the greatest gift that God made to man, in the words of Dante, compelling as ever, "was the freedom of the will / with which all creatures of intellect / and they alone, were and are endowed."[161]

11. Grace, or Created Wisdom

From the standpoint of created goods, however, the highest good of the universe is not freedom, but that which Scripture calls created wisdom.

---

[159] Card. Charles Journet, *Per una teologia ecclesiale della storia della salvezza*, tr. Ital. D'Auria, Napoli 1972, pp. 128–129.

[160] St. Thomas Aquinas, *De Veritate*, q. 22, a. 2, ad 5.

[161] Dante Alighieri, Paradiso, c. 5, vv. 21–24.

In fact, Scripture asserts that "before all other things wisdom was created" (Sir. 1:4). This created wisdom can be understood as the created nature, body and soul, of Jesus Christ, distinct from His divine nature, although united to it in one person, the incarnate Word or uncreated wisdom. But created wisdom is also, according to the theologians, the created grace whose foundation and source is Jesus Christ, Uncreated Grace. There is no contradiction between the two realities. For created grace is no different from Jesus Christ Himself who communicates Himself to souls, lifting them up to the supernatural plane.

Just as the soul is the vital principle of the body, grace is the vital principle of the soul. Without the supernatural influence of grace, the soul is deprived of true life. Grace, according to the definition of St. Peter, is the communicative participation in the divine nature (2 Pet. 1:3–4). St. Thomas defines it as "an influence of divine Goodness in the soul,"[162] which "bestows upon the spiritual creature a certain participation in the very nature of God."[163] Grace, then, is a free and supernatural gift which flows out from the Goodness of God, and which lifts human nature to participation with the divine nature. It is called "created" not on account of its

---

[162] St. Thomas Aquinas, Opusc. 51, *De Sacram*, c. 26.

[163] Id., *Summa Theologiae*, III, q. 62, a. 1.

substance, which is supernatural, but rather because it is a finite good which comes from God. As a supernatural good, however, grace transcends and overcomes all created nature. For this reason, St. Thomas could write that "the smallest degree of participation in sanctifying grace, considered in a single individual, is superior to the natural good of the entire universe," and it is a greater thing to guide a sinner back into a state of grace than to create Heaven and earth.[164]

Grace, St. Thomas states, is brought about in man by the presence of divinity, just as light in the air is the result of the presence of the sun.[165] It is an active principle which comes not from man, but from God Himself.

The Council of Trent defines grace as a gift of God which comes before every human merit.[166] God, who alone is good, acts in the hearts of men and in free will itself such that only through Him can we do any good.[167] God, singular cause of the good of the universe, brings about the movement of grace in man, enlightening, inspiring, and moving his will. But man, via his freedom, may cause his soul to move toward God because God requires

[164] Ibid., I–II, q. 113, a. 9, ad 2.

[165] Ibid., III, q. 7, a. 13.

[166] Council of Trent, *Decree concerning Justification*, in Denz-H, nn. 1532–33.

[167] Denz-H, n. 244.

the free cooperation of man and grace will not bring about good without the freedom of the creature.

If freedom makes us capable of moving toward our singular good, grace causes all the good in us that we are capable of. Grace is a supernatural quality that imprints itself on our souls, permeates all our faculties, and transforms our lives.

There is an endless number of created graces bestowed by divine goodness throughout the ages. Their number is greater than the stars in the sky and the droplets of water in the ocean. Every grace is unique, just as every star differs from every other, and, as St. Francis de Sales writes, this variety in grace — or this grace in variety — "constitutes a holy beauty and the sweetest harmony that delights the whole of the Holy City of Heavenly Jerusalem."[168]

12. Jesus Christ and His Mystical Body

Jesus Christ, Uncreated Grace, conveys Himself to souls under the form of created grace, of sanctifying influence, of supernatural life. He is the universal fount of every grace, as God is the supreme source of every being. In this sense, there is nothing in the universe apart from Jesus Christ, the God-Man, Redeemer of humanity. Jesus Christ is the Alpha and Omega,

---

[168] St. Francis De Sales, *Trattato dell'Amor di Dio*, pp. 200–201.

the beginning and end of all things (Rev. 1:8). In Him, the work of creation finds its fulfillment and the fullness of its significance. "Christ is at the center of creatures just as the sun among the planets, like the heart of His creation, conveying light, life, and motion to all its members and acting as their center of gravity so that in Him and through Him they may rest in the midst of God."[169]

With the complete offer of Himself to God, the incarnate Word became sacrificial victim, redeemed men, freed him from the slavery of sin, and reestablished the reign of grace that the sin of Adam had destroyed. In this sense, the Mystery of the Cross is the most perfect expression of divine love which unites Heaven and earth: perfect Love of the Son of God for man and perfect Love of the Son of God for the Father.

Jesus Christ could have redeemed countless worlds with one drop of blood, or even with only a tear. But in the Crucifixion, as says St. Thomas, God "showed a greater mercy than if he had remitted sins without payment — without the pouring out of the Blood of Christ."[170] For by dying Jesus Christ wished to embrace, not sin, which diametrically opposed His

---

169   Matthias J. Scheeben, *I misteri del cristianesimo*, tr. Ital. Morcelliana, Brescia 1953, p. 318.

170   St. Thomas Aquinas, *Summa Theologiae*, III, q. 46, a. 1, ad 3.

perfection, but the physical consequences that it entailed for humanity: dishonor, pain, and death.

The hill of Calvary is the apex of history. Jesus Christ, from this height, stands above all that was and all that will be created from the beginning of time. An inexhaustible river of supernatural graces flows forth from this hill, pouring out to all times and all places through the eucharistic sacrifice of the Mass, which bloodlessly renews the divine sacrifice of the Cross.[171] The infinite love of God reaches the furthest limits in the Eucharist, in which He nourishes the members of His Mystical Body with His Body and Blood.[172]

The Mystical Body is like an extension of the life of Jesus Christ in time and space, who by assuming His human nature in the most pure womb of Mary has indescribably united all mankind to Himself forever, and by dying on Calvary, He has redeemed it, forming with it a mysterious organism, of which the human body is a distant image. All men partake notionally in this mystical organism, but they become members of it in deed by Baptism, which is the Sacrament of Faith. There is order,

---

[171] Council of Trent, Session 22a, *De SS. Missæ Sacrificio*, in Denz-H, n. 1740.

[172] Conrad Algermissen, *La Chiesa cattolica e le altre chiese cattoliche*, tr. Ital., Edizioni Paoline, Roma 1960, p. 278.

proportion, and subordination within the structure of this organism, the Holy Church: each member has a vital function that contributes to the life of the whole organism.[173]

The ultimate end of the Church, just like that of the whole universe, is the glory of God, of whom she herself is a veiled representation, because in her is made manifest the glory of Christ, which is poured into her by the Holy Spirit (John 17:10–22). This manifestation is "veiled," observes Fr. Schmaus, insofar as the Church, the Mystical Body of Christ, does not exist on the earth in the form of glory, but rather in the form of the Cross.[174] All the evil that can be found in the Church is outside of it and comes from the world; all the good found within the world is divine and comes from the Church, which is holy and immaculate in its faith, in its Sacraments, in the sanctity of life of those whom it puts forth as models.

"The beauty of God," writes Plinio Corrêa de Oliveira:

> Is reflected in the hierarchical and harmonious whole of all beings, such that, in a certain sense, there is no better means of getting to

---

173 Card. Pietro Parente, *Nel mistero di Cristo*, Belardetti, Roma 1995, p. 92.

174 Michele Schmaus s.j., *Dogmatica cattolica*, tr. Ital., Marietti, Torino 1959, vol. III/1, p. 562.

know the infinite and uncreated beauty of God than by analyzing the finite and created beauty of the universe, considering it not so much in each particular being as much as in its entirety. But God is also reflected in a higher and more perfect masterpiece of the cosmos: It is the Mystical Body of Christ, the supernatural society that we venerate with the name of Holy Roman Catholic Apostolic Church. She herself constitutes an entire universe of harmonious and varied aspects that sing and reflect, each in its own way, the indescribable and holy beauty of God and of the incarnate Word. By contemplating on the one hand the universe, and on the other the Holy Church, we can rise to the level of meditation upon the holy, infinite, uncreated beauty of God.[175]

The eternal plans of God converge toward a historical reality, the Church, which is Jesus Christ Himself living and working in history and within humanity. The Church Militant on Earth — together with the Church Penitent in Purgatory and the Church Triumphant in Heaven — forms the one Church of Christ. Indeed St. Augustine says, "all the

[175] Plinio Corrêa de Oliveira, *A inocência primiera e a contemplação sacral*, Artpress, São Paulo 2008, p. 98.

Church forms one body in Christ."[176] The Church Militant is a mysterious reality, simultaneously temporal and eternal: human by virtue of the members who compose it, and divine by virtue of its origin, end, and means. In defining it, "nothing can be found which is more noble, more sublime, or more divine than that expression which is called *the Mystical Body of Christ*."[177]

By the will of her founder, the Church is a visible society composed of different members connected to one another organically to pursue the same end. But in a far more intimate and perfect manner than a simple social body, she is united by a supernatural principle that is the same divine Spirit which "one and identical in number, fills and unites the whole Church."[178] There is no contrast between the visible, juridical dimension of the Church and her invisible, supernatural dimension. "The totality and union of these two parts," asserts Leo XIII, "is altogether necessary to the Church as the intimate union of soul and body is to human nature."[179] The divine will has endowed the Church with universal absolute power and governing authority that constitutes the principle

---

[176] St. Augustine, *Enarrationes in Psalmos*, n. 148.
[177] Pius XII, *Mystici corporis Christi*, June 29, 1943.
[178] St. Thomas Aquinas, *De Veritate*, q. 29, a. 4.
[179] Leo XIII, *Satis cognitum*, June 29, 1896.

of unity of her social life.[180] *Ubi Petrus, ibi Ecclesia*. The papacy sums up and encapsulates in itself the whole Catholic Church.

The Church is the continuation and the drawing out of incarnate Wisdom, which enacts in individuals, just as in humanity as a whole, the work of Redemption and brings the Kingdom of God about in a hierarchical, organized, social form in souls and society. Established by Jesus Christ, Son of God, the Church is His living continuation throughout the ages. She exercises her mission by bringing into conformity with the Law of Christ not only individuals, but also peoples, nations, governments, and all human society, over which the absolute sovereignty of our Lord is exercised.

Society, which in its spirit, customs, and laws conforms itself to the principles of the Church, has earned the title Christian civilization. Pius X, in his encyclical *Il Fermo Proposito*, reiterated that "the civilization of the world is Christian. The more completely Christian it is, the more true, more lasting and more productive of genuine fruit it is,"[181] and in the letter, *Notre Charge Apostolique*, recalls that "civilization does not need to be invented, nor must a new society be built among the clouds. It

---

[180] Card. Alfonso Maria Stickler, *Il mistero della Chiesa nel Diritto Canonico*, in Aa. Vv., Il mistero della Chiesa, Paoline, Roma 1962, p. 277.

[181] St. Pius X, *Il Fermo Proposito,* June 11, 1905.

is established and exists: It is Christian civilization. It is Catholic society. It consists only in unceasingly establishing and restoring it in its natural and divine foundations, against renewed attacks of unhealthy utopia, revolution, and impiety: *Omnia instaurare in Christo* (Eph. 1:10)."[182]

Christendom was the first historical expression of the perennial model of Christian civilization. It is, according to Plinio Corrêa de Oliveira, "a projection, in the natural field, of that great supernatural reality that is the Mystical Body of our Lord Jesus Christ."[183]

When a society is Christian, it reflects to a higher degree the glory of God, Lord of the Universe. There is nothing in creation that is not entirely in the hands of God and subject to Him. Before Him, every man must confess: "You made Heaven and earth and every wonderful thing under Heaven. You are Lord of all" (Esther 4:3–4).

13. The Sacred Heart of Jesus

The ladder of creatures leads even higher toward Jesus Christ, incarnate Word, second Person of the Most Holy Trinity.

---

182 Id., *Notre Charge Apostolique* August 25, 1910.
183 P. Corrêa de Oliveira, *Cristandade*, "O Legionário", n. 732 (18 agosto 1946); cfr. anche Civilização cristã, "O Legionário", n. 546 (24 gennaio 1943).

Jesus Christ is not a creature, just as the term *creature* cannot define His Mystical Body, the Church.

Jesus Christ is not a creature because in Him the divine nature, uniting itself with human nature, consisting in union of body and soul, forms a single uncreated Person. In Him, there is a true body and true soul, yet at the same time also perfect divinity. These three substances, says St. Thomas Aquinas, are united in one singular uncreated Person.[184]

Jesus Christ is not a creature because He has only one Person, and this Person is uncreated and is one in two natures, "by which we do not state that Christ is a creature, because, speaking in absolutes, this name refers to the hypostasis: nevertheless we speak of the soul of Christ or His body as creations."[185] Similarly, we cannot define the Church as a "creature," because she constitutes a body whose head is a divine and uncreated Person, and in her, alongside human reality, an uncreated and divine reality coexists mysteriously.

The soul of Christ, however, is a creature, and everything in Christ that belongs to human nature is created; otherwise in Him, the nature of His humanity would not be different from His divinity. The Apostle Paul seemed to refer to this creatureliness of His nature when he defines Him as "the

---

[184] St. Thomas Aquinas, *Compendium Theologiae*, I, cap. 209, n. 402.
[185] Ibid., I, cap. 216, n. 436.

firstborn of all creation. For in Him were created all things in Heaven and on earth" (Col. 1:15–17). In this respect, it is correct to say that there is no creature higher than the human nature of Christ, and that in this nature, composed of body and soul, what is highest is His soul, filled to the brim with grace such that it can be called created grace itself, for there is no grace that is not contained within it. In this same sense, St. Thomas states, "the soul of Christ is the most excellent of all creatures."[186] For it "has infinite and limitless grace by virtue of the fact that it has united itself to the Word, which is the inexhaustible and infinite source and principle of all the issuing forth of the creatures."[187]

The same adoration that is owed to the divine Person of the Redeemer is owed to the human nature of Christ, composed of His body and soul, not for its own sake, but insofar as it is united to the Divine Word. In the Person of Jesus Christ, the most excellent part is His Sacred Heart, fount of His immense love, "the legitimate symbol of that unbounded love. Under the influence of this love, our Savior, by the outpouring of His blood, became wedded to His Church."[188]

[186] Ibid., I, cap. 216, n. 439.
[187] Ibid., I, cap. 215, n. 432.
[188] Pius XII, *Haurietis Aquas*, May 15, 1956.

The cult of the Sacred Heart of Jesus has as its proper and ultimate focus, not only the physical heart of Jesus, though the noblest part of His humanity, but also His soul and His divinity, that is, the whole Person of our Lord, adored in His two natures, divine and human. The human nature of Christ, then, is adored not in and for itself, as is the case with God, but in view of the Word to which it is hypostatically united.[189]

In the cult of the Sacred Heart, defined by Pius XII as "the synthesis of the whole mystery of our redemption" and "the practical profession of all of Christianity,"[190] we can admire the encapsulation, in a certain sense, of the entire Christian religion, which is the religion of God's infinite love for mankind.[191]

14. The Immaculate Heart of Mary, Summit of Creation

The highest perfection that a creature can attain is not that of nature, but that of personhood, inasmuch as a person can take on nature and not vice versa.[192] In this respect, we must say that there is no created person in the universe more excellent

---

[189] Card. P. Parente, *Unione ipostatica*, in Enciclopedia Cattolica, Editrice Vaticana, Roma 1950, vol. XII, col. 824.

[190] Pius XII, *Haurietis Aquas*, cit.

[191] Card. P. Parente, *Dio e i Problemi dell'Uomo*, Belardetti, Roma 1955, pp. 464–65.

[192] St. Thomas Aquinas, *Summa Theologiae*, I, q. 29, aa. 1,3.

than Mary, the human person who begot the Divine Word. It is true that the person and nature of Mary are created, unlike the Person of Jesus Christ who is unique in having two natures and yet being uncreated. In this sense, it is right to affirm with St. Maximilian Kolbe that "the Immaculate Mary is the highest grade of perfection and sanctity of creation,"[193] and to say, with St. Louis-Marie Grignion de Montfort, that "Mary is the excellent masterpiece of the Most High."[194]

By Himself alone and through Himself alone, as the incarnate Word, Jesus Christ possesses an incomprehensible and infinite fullness of grace. But Divine Providence wished to communicate the fullness of grace of the God-Man to a simple creature, elevating her to the almost infinite dignity of Mother of the incarnate Word.[195] Mary, by whom the Word was born according to the Flesh,[196] gave body and life to the Author of every grace and for this reason is called *Mater Divinae Gratiae*. All graces communicated to the angels and

---

[193] S. Massimiliano Kolbe, Conferenza del 3 luglio 1938, cit. in H. M. Manteau-Bonamy, O.P., *Lo Spirito Santo e l'Immacolata*, Centro Internazionale Milizia Immacolata, Roma 1983, p. 87.

[194] St. Louis-Marie Grignion de Montfort, *Trattato della vera Devozione alla Vergine Maria*, nn. 5, 20.

[195] St. Thomas Aquinas, *Summa Theologiae*, I, q. 25, a. 6, ad 4; S. Alfonso Maria de' Liguori, *Le glorie di Maria*, Redentoristi, Roma 1937, pp. 94–97.

[196] Concilio di Efeso, in Denz-H, n. 251.

mankind, from the beginning of creation until the end of the world, in their number, diversity, and intensity, are gathered and concentrated in Mary Most Holy, whom Divine Providence wished to institute as treasurer and dispenser of all graces. On this Leo XIII states "Accordingly, it can be affirmed with all truth and precision that, by divine disposition, nothing of the limitless treasury of the graces of Christ can be communicated to us except through Mary."[197]

From the first moment of her existence, as we read in the papal bull *Ineffabilis Deus*, which defines the Immaculate Conception, Mary was replete with light, beauty, and holiness and was placed above all the angels and saints. St. Alphonsus, citing Sts. Ephrem and Andrew of Crete, writes that nothing, except God, is higher than her in the universe.[198] St. Anselm agrees, saying "Nothing is equal to Mary: Nothing, except God, is greater than Mary."[199] According to St. Bernardino of Siena, she is so far above that only God can and indeed does understand her.[200] The reason for this is evident to St. Thomas: the closer something gets to its principle, i.e., its

[197] Leo XIII, *Octobri Mense*, Sept. 22, 1891.

[198] S. Alfonso M. de' Liguori, *Le Glorie di Maria*, cit., p. 92.

[199] S. Anselmo, *Oratio* 52, in PL, 158, col. 956.

[200] S. Bernardino da Siena, Sermo V, *De Nativitate B.M.V.*, cap. 12, cit. in S. Alfonso M. de' Liguori, *Le Glorie di Maria*, cit., p. 93.

origin, the more it receives from its perfection.[201] For this reason, St. Denis the Carthusian asserts that there is nothing more perfect than the Mother of God, except the hypostatic union.[202] "Accordingly, there can be no doubt," states Pius XII, "that Mary surpasses in dignity all of creation and holds primacy over all after her son."[203] As Maximilian Kolbe writes, in her, the miracle of the union of all creation with God is accomplished: "Love joins not only these two persons, but the first of them is all the love of the Most Holy Trinity and the second is all the love of creation, and so in this union Heaven is joined to the earth, all of Heaven with all of earth, all eternal love with all created love: It is the summit of love!"[204] This is why the Church reserves to the Most Holy Virgin the special veneration of hyperdulia, which has as its object her person and her heart.

As in Jesus Christ, so too in Mary, there is no part more excellent and more noble than the heart. In Mary's heart, states St. Louis-Marie Grignion de Montfort, God Himself

---

[201] St. Thomas Aquinas, *Summa Theologiae*, III, q. 27, a. 5.

[202] S. Dionigi Cartusianus, *De Dignitate et laudibus B.M.V.*, cit. in S. Alfonso M. de' Liguori, *Le Glorie di Maria*, cit., p. 95.

[203] Pius XII, Enciclica sulla *Regalità di Maria SS.ma* dell'11 ottobre 1954.

[204] Cit. in Giorgio Domanski, *Il pensiero mariano di P. Massimiliano Kolbe*, L.E.M.I., Roma 1971, p. 45.

has taken up residence with all His perfections.[205] The Immaculate Heart is, as the Fathers say, "the seat of divine secrets,"[206] the treasure of the universe, the tabernacle which guards all created goods. The Word, writes Hugh of Saint Victor, came down into the womb of Mary precisely because it was conceived first in her heart.[207]

The womb of Mary was the point of union between Heaven and earth, between God and man, between Him who is and him who is not. The ladder which leads the created world to God had in this "sealed fount" (Song of Sol. 4:12), in this terrestrial paradise, in this great and divine world,[208] its sublime summit. God descended to man through Mary, and through Mary man may ascend back to God. "The Most High divinely and perfectly descended to us through humble Mary, without losing any of His divinity or holiness. And it is through Mary that the smallest ones must climb perfectly and divinely to the Most High, without fear."[209] The most pure heart of Mary represents in this sense the supreme created good, the masterpiece of the

---

205 St. Louis-Marie Grignion de Montfort, *Trattato della vera Devozione*, n. 178.

206 Ibid., nn. 248, 264.

207 Hugh of Saint Victor, *De Beatae Mariae virginitate*, n. 2.

208 St. Louis-Marie Grignion de Montfort, *Trattato della vera Devozione*, n. 6.

209 Ibid., n. 157.

hands of Divine Providence, to be contemplated in silence for the incomprehensible miracles that God has worked in it. At Fátima, our Lady, in person, infallibly promised the triumph of the Immaculate Heart of Mary over contemporary chaos.

PART THREE

Disorder and Its Meaning

1. Order and Chaos: The Two Poles of the Universe

There is a ladder which leads the created world to God, but
there is also a ladder which tragically leads away from Him.
For in the universe, hierarchically ordered by Divine Providence, there also exists disorder by divine decree, which has
its own scale of gradations. There is a profound and irreconcilable difference between the two scales of order: one that
ascends from the lowest degrees of being up to the transcendent first principle of the universe and the other that progressively descends and retreats from it.

The ladder of good is the ontological hierarchy of created perfections which reaches from creatures without reason to rational creatures: goodness corresponds to Being in
increasingly intense and perfect degrees. It reaches its apex
in the person of Mary, Mother of created wisdom, that is

Mother of the incarnate Word and of all the graces of which He is the source.

The ladder of evil and disorder, present in rational creatures alone, is a hierarchy of retreat from Being, not ontological, but rather moral, because it presupposes the possibility of choice by the creature, its refusal of the good, and its opting for evil. In irrational creatures, there is no evil, only degrees of greater or lesser perfections according to their perfect nature in and of itself, as specific nature. In rational creatures, however, free will puts before man the fundamental choice between divine order and infernal chaos.

Disorder is the absence or refusal of every order, law, or principle by the rational creature. In a word, it is anarchy. In its deepest sense, anarchy is, as Donoso Cortés states, "the denial of order, or rather of the divine affirmation relative to the mode of being of all things."[210] "Considering that there is no species of good except order," writes the great Spanish thinker, "that which exists outside of order can be nothing other than evil. Nor is there any species of evil that does not reside outside of order; for this reason, just as order is the supreme good, so too disorder is evil par excellence. Outside of disorder there is no evil, just as outside of order there is no good."[211]

---

[210] J. Donoso Cortés, *Saggio sul cattolicesimo*, cit., p. 180.
[211] Ibid., p. 204.

Disorder is chaos. Chaos is the deprivation of order, but seeing as order is a good in and of itself, chaos, which is the absence of the perfection of order, cannot then be a good nor exist in itself. If it were so, it would be possible to think of a perfect and absolute chaos, analogous and opposed to absolute order. In this case, chaos would cease to be as such, but would either coincide with nothingness or with the order that it would attempt to oppose, in the same way that disease is a deficiency of order, but not of everything. For, as St. Dionysius the Areopagite observes, "if disorder were complete, there would not even be disease. Disease remains and is present insofar as it has the least substance of order and subsists in this piece."[212] In absolute chaos, however one wishes to imagine it, it would mean the end and the negation of chaos itself.

In reality, chaos exists not for its own sake, but only as mere deprivation of order, "for that which is completely deprived of the good is not a being and cannot remain among beings."[213] Chaos, then, is not a positive reality, but is privative, which always presupposes the order to which to attach itself, just as sickness needs the human body to develop and ceases to exist when its host dies. Disorder, like

[212] Dionysius the Areopagite, *De Divinis Nominibus*, IV, 20, 720c.
[213] Ibid.

evil, "is not a part of the universe," asserts St. Thomas Aquinas, precisely because "its nature is neither of substance, nor of accident, but only of privation."[214] "Then, to sum up," writes St. Dionysius again, "the good derives from a single and complete cause, while evil derives from many and individual deficiencies."[215]

2. Physical Evil and Moral Evil

According to the Angelic Doctor, the evil in created things is "the deprivation of the good" that is owed to their nature.[216] And since the good of which a creature can be deprived is either physical or moral, so too can evil be physical or moral.

Physical evil is the deprivation of those goods that constitute or complement the physical perfection of a being. This could arise in all living creatures, both rational and irrational. In living beings, physical evil is represented most of all by suffering and death, which is the highest physical evil because it constitutes the dissolution of matter. All creatures, rational and irrational, suffer physical evil without willing it. For this reason, physical evil in humans, even though it may feel like suffering punishment, is never a

[214] St. Thomas Aquinas, *In II Sent.*, d, 46, q. 1, a. 3.

[215] Dionysius the Areopagite, *De Divinis Nominibus*, IV, 30, 732a.

[216] St. Thomas Aquinas, *Summa Theologiae*, I, q. 14, a. 10.

moral fault unless it is born of their free will. It may become one when it is inflicted on oneself or on others.

Moral evil is the deprivation of that good which consists in conforming the rational creature's will to the divine order. Unlike physical evil, this presupposes the responsibility and therefore the fault of the creature because it is produced by a distancing of the will from the eternal law. The first roots of this evil are always in the limitation of the created being, accentuated by Original Sin.

Theologians label moral evils as "*malum culpae*" and all physical evils of the universe as "*malum paenae.*" Moral evils are not only more intense and graver, but more numerous and extensive than physical evils, even though human sensibilities are especially affected by the latter.[217] Physical evils and moral evils, however, are always connected. "Besides," notes Donoso Cortés, "it could not be any different, given that the physical and the moral both find their origin and end in God."[218]

The double order of fault and punishment, writes St. Bonaventure, governs all things to the point that every fault necessarily falls back into punishment.[219] Every moral

[217] Ibid., I, q. 63, a. 9.

[218] J. Donoso Cortés, *Saggio sul cattolicesimo*, cit., p. 191.

[219] St. Bonaventure, *Breviloquium*, parte III, cap. IV, n. 2.

evil is ascribed solely to man and in this sense is a true evil; every physical evil is ascribed to God and cannot be understood as evil because God causes only the good. The *malum paenae* is not evil in an absolute sense, only rather in some respects, while in the absolute it must be understood as a good.[220]

However, as St. Augustine observes, the blessedness of order is such that the deformity of the fault cannot subsist for one moment without the beauty of recompense and retribution: "He who does not render to God that which he owes Him by doing as much as he should, renders it to Him by suffering what he must. There is no middle way. ... The beauty of universal order is such that it cannot tolerate for even one moment being stained by the ugliness of sin, without being touched up by the beauty of retribution."[221]

Every wrong calls for a punishment, and every punishment is firstly retributive as justice demands. But it is also remedial according to the designs of divine mercy. The supreme meeting point between justice and mercy was worked within the person of the Redeemer and accomplished upon the Cross.[222]

---

[220] St. Thomas Aquinas, *Summa Theologiae*, II–II, q. 19, a. 1.

[221] St. Augustine, *De libero arbitrio*, 3, 44.

[222] F. Pollien, *La vita interiore semplificata*, cit., pp. 419–20.

3. Sin Is the Singular Evil in the Universe

The world seems to overflow with evils, yet there is only one. The only true evil possible in the universe is the moral evil willed by the rational creature because this alone turns the creature from the singular Supreme Good that is God. The retreat of the rational creature from God is an evil that is properly defined as "sin." Sin is constituted, according to St. Augustine, by every word, act, or desire that is contrary to the eternal law of God, which constitutes the supreme order of the universe.[223]

Sin can be defined as the disorder of the will which is not conformed to the divine order, breaking the relationship which unites it to its principle: the creature places its will and its pleasure, whether intellectual or sensory, before the glory of its Creator.

Sin is disorder par excellence. In this sense, just as there is only one good, which is God, His law and His glory, there exists only one evil, sin, which is the affront to God's glory. It consists in the deliberate violation of divine order and rule. Sin is the singular and absolute evil of creation because it directly opposes God, who is the singular cause and supreme good of the universe. The glory of God, Fr. Pollien

[223] St. Augustine, *Contra Faustum Manicheum*, XXII, 27.

reminds us, is therefore singular, universal good, the source and motive for every good; sin is the singular, universal evil, source and motive for every evil.[224]

God alone is eternal, and nothing subsists on anything without reference to Him. Sin, which represents the absolute evil, properly does not exist. For it does not exist in itself, but only in the free creature that commits it. Sin, notes Fr. Scheeben, has no cause, but a non-cause, or rather a *"causa deficiens."*[225] The paradox of evil, writes Cardinal Journet, is that is exists without being: it exists, but only insofar as a deprivation of a good, that is, as an accident, not as a real substance.[226]

Sin does not have being in itself because God, who is the highest good and essential Being, has not created anything bad or imperfect within the universe.[227] Every creature, insofar as it exists, is good, because with its being it receives from God its own degree of goodness. This goodness constitutes its own proper perfection. Nothing created

[224] F. Pollien, *La vita interiore semplificata*, cit., p. 137.
[225] M. Scheeben, *I misteri del cristianesimo*, cit., p. 184.
[226] Card. Charles Journet, *Le mal*. Essai théologique, Desclée, de Brouwer, Paris 1962, pp. 48–49.
[227] St. Thomas Aquinas, *Compendium Theologiae*, I, cap. 115, n. 224; *Summa Theologiae*, I, q. 48, a. 1; *De Malo*, q. 1, a. 1; *De Divinis Nominibus*, c. 4, I, 14.

by God can be in itself bad. For this reason, as St. Augustine states, evil is not a substance, because if it were it would be good.[228] The evil of sin therefore does not trace back to the creative action of God, but has its cause, insofar as it is disordered, in the de-creative action of man.

It is true, explains St. Thomas, that God, as pure act, is the cause in the universe of every action as action.[229] But sin entails a defective act, devoid of perfection; this defect does not originate from God, but from the free will of the rational creature, which shirks the divine order. No one, then, except the sinner, can be the cause of the sin committed. This is why God is the cause of all that happens in the universe besides sin.

God is the first cause of all the good that we work; rational creatures are the sole cause of the evil that they commit when their will retreats from God, the highest and singular good. Rational creatures — free, but imperfect — can stray from the perfectly ordered creator-will that has placed it in existence. That which turns them away from the divine will is sin. The singular cause of sin is the disordered will of the sinner that resists the divine will. For God does not retreat from His creatures, and sin is

---

[228] St. Augustine, *Confessiones*, libro VII, cap. 12, n. 8.

[229] St. Thomas Aquinas, *Summa Theologiae*, I–II, q. 49, a. 2.

possible only to the extent that they retreat from Him.[230] For this reason, St. Augustine says: "Love what God has made, hate what you have made."[231] Every created good comes from God, the supreme Good; every evil and disorder of the universe comes from creatures.

The only creatures that can sin are rational creatures, namely, the angels and men, because these alone, made in the image and likeness of their Maker, are endowed with intelligence and freedom and may disobey and rebel against divine law.

Conformity to the will of God is the supreme act of love of the rational creatures; cosmic disorder is the inevitable consequence of their sin.

4. Original Sin and Its Consequences

"Through one person sin entered the world, and through sin, death, and thus death came to all, inasmuch as all sinned" (Rom. 5:12). All the disorder and evils of the world trace their source to the Original Sin transmitted by Adam to humanity. "In the dynamics of Original Sin," comments St. Thomas, "there is order: First, Adam corrupted nature with the act of his sin. Then, the corruption of nature falls back

---

[230] Id., *In II Sent.*, d. 37, q. 2, a. 1, ad 3.
[231] St. Augustine, *Enarrationes in Psalmos*, 44, n. 18.

upon the person. Finally, this nature is transmitted to others by a sinful person."[232]

Adam and Eve had received numerous gifts, both supernatural and natural, from God as a hereditary gift, transmissible to their descendants. This good, the Angelic Doctor explains, "was given to the first man not as to an individual person, but as to the first principle of human nature, through which it would be transmitted alongside human nature to his descendants."[233] This did not happen, however, on account of the disobedience of the ancestors.

It is a dogma of faith, defined by a number of councils.[234] Adam and Eve gravely sinned by disobeying a divine command. The divine sentence resulting from the sin became the law of humanity. With grace destroyed within himself, Adam could no longer transmit it to his children. To them he would pass on not supernatural life, but spiritual death. Sin passed from ancestors to all descendants, with the exception of the Virgin Mary, chosen by Divine Providence to cooperate with Jesus Christ in the redemption of humanity from sin.

[232] St. Thomas Aquinas, *In II Sent.*, d. 31, q. 1, a. 1.

[233] Id., *Compendium theologiae*, I, cap. 187, n. 364; cf. *Summa Theologiae*, I, q. 102, a. 2; *II Sent.*, d, 29, a. 5.

[234] Cfr. ad es. Concilio di Trento, *Decreto sul peccato originale*, in DENZ-H, n. 510.

With Adam, all of humanity became sinful, just as in Christ it was redeemed. All humanity is summed up, states St. Augustine, "in the story of two men, one lost us in him, doing his own will and not that of Him who had created Him. The other, instead saved us in him, doing not his own will, but that of Him who had sent him. In the history of these two is the whole of the Christian faith."[235]

Original Sin was a rift between man and God that wounded both the soul and the body of man, producing a moral disorder resulting in a physical disorder culminating in death. God had created man as immortal; after sin, human life was, as St. Augustine says, "a race toward death."[236] Death is the indelible seal that expresses the loss of the supernatural life endured by man as a result of the wrong of his ancestors. It is the supreme physical evil, following from the moral evil of sin. The gravest consequence of the sin of Adam was not the introduction of the death of the body, but the introduction of the death of the soul, the rupture of the sublime relationship that God held with the reasoning creature.

Death, disease, suffering, anguish, error, doubt, conflict: all of this followed Original Sin:

[235] St. Augustine, *De gratia Christi et de peccato originali*, Lib. II, c. 24.
[236] Id., *De Civitate Dei*, XIII, 10.

Sin covered Heaven with mourning, Hell with flames, and the earth with thistles; it brought sickness and plague, and famine and death to the world; it dug the grave of the most illustrious and populous cities, it presided over the funerals of Babylon, the city of sumptuous gardens, and of Nineveh the proud, of Persepolis the daughter of the sun, of Memphis of the profound mysteries, of Sodom the lascivious, of Athens the cradle of art, of Jerusalem the thankless, of Rome the great; for God, if He willed these things, He willed them only as the punishment and remedy of sin. Sin is responsible for the groans that rise from men's breasts and the tears that trickle drop by drop from men's eyes. But the even graver aspect of sin, which no intellect can conceive and no words express, is that it was able to draw tears from the most holy eyes of the Son of God, the meek lamb who ascended the Cross burdened with the sins of the world. Neither the Heavens nor the earth nor man saw Him smile, but they saw Him weep; and He wept because He had fixed His eyes on sin. He wept over the tomb of Lazarus, and in the death of His friend He wept over nothing more than the death of the sinful soul. He shed tears over Jerusalem, and the cause of His weeping lay in the abominable sin of the deicidal people. He knew in the Garden sadness and turmoil, and the horror of sin was the cause of that uncharacteristic turmoil and that unusual sadness. His forehead sweated blood, and the specter of sin was the cause of that strange sweat. He was nailed to a piece of wood, and it was sin that nailed Him there; it was sin that gave Him agony, sin that gave Him death.[237]

5.   God Brings Good from Evil

Without Original Sin, one cannot comprehend how the earth could be a vale of tears and how all the tragedy and suffering that runs through it could be the result of man's disordered will. However, the physical and moral disorder introduced into the world by Original Sin fits into the grand plan of creation, planned and willed by God from eternity.

God is the first and universal cause of all things, and everything that happens is willed by Him, except sin, which He permits but does not will. God does not cause, but permits, the moral evil of sin because, in His infinite wisdom, goodness, and power, He knows, wills, and can draw good out from evil, order out from disorder. "The evil that God does not will," writes St. Augustine, "is not outside the rational law that God wills. For He wills that the good should be

[237] J. Donoso Cortés, *Saggio sul cattolicesimo*, cit., pp. 211–212.

desired and evil not desired; which is the essence of the rationality of the whole and of the divine order."[238]

God allows evil not in the sense that He puts up with it but rather because He wishes to allow it.[239] "God does not wish for evils to exist; neither does he wish that no evils should exist: but he wishes to allow that there may be evils. And this is good."[240] Indeed, according to St. Augustine, He has deemed it better to allow the existence of evil in order to draw good from it than to avoid the existence of any evil whatsoever.[241] To derive good from evil is to know how to bring about good by means of that evil which occurs without its being willed as such. God, however, does not will evil in order to bring about a better good, but exclusively wills a better good that requires that evil for its realization.

If God had not allowed evil and sin, the spiritual being would have been deprived of the gift of freedom that makes him a participant in divine causality, "the principle of his own work as God is."[242] This participation of man in divine causality cannot be absolute, for it would make man another God; being relative and imperfect, it implies the possibility

---

[238] St. Augustine, *De Ordine*, I, 7, 18.

[239] Card. C. Journet, *Le mal*, cit., p. 87.

[240] St. Thomas Aquinas, *Summa Theologiae*, I, q. 2, a. 3, ad 1.

[241] St. Augustine, *Enchiridion*, XXVII, n. 8.

[242] St. Thomas Aquinas, *Summa Theologiae*, I–IIae, Prolog.

of fault, that is, of disordered use of the gift of freedom. "It is the law of the living state that divine grace can be rejected. God beseeches us to be preferred but allows that we may offend Him. He can be permanently preferred: this is the story of the man who enters Paradise at the last moment (Luke 23:43); but he can also be permanently rejected: this is the story of the man for whom it would have been better never to have been born (Matt. 24:26)."[243]

If God had not, by analogy, contributed a degree of His freedom to man and angel, He would have deprived them of the greatest of the gifts they received. God is love: His infinite love, and that alone, was the cause of the gift of freedom, which carried with it the possibility of sin because of man's inevitably imperfect and finite nature.[244]

Divine love, which allowed sin, orders it to a higher good because everything in the universe cooperates with the good, and God is always victorious, in time and eternity.

All the evils that God permits, writes St. Thomas, are ordered to a good: not always, however, to the good of the one who endures them, but sometimes they are ordered to the good of others, or of the whole universe. "In this way

---

[243] Card. C. Journet, *Per una teologia ecclesiale della storia della salvezza*, cit., p. 131.

[244] St. Bonaventure, *In II Sent.*, dist. 34, art. 1, q. 2.

God has so ordained the sin of tyrants to the good of martyrs and the pains of the damned to the glorification of his righteousness."[245] The hill of Calvary upon which the deicide took place represents the culmination of evil achieved in history, but also the supreme fount of good that has flowed out from it over the centuries until the end of the world. Only the Cross can give us the key to the mystery of evil and pain. "Every eye that Calvary has not illuminated," Dom Pollien observes, "remains blind to this point."[246]

The reason for the sufferings of the One who was called "*vir dolorum*" (Isa. 53:9) is the reason, and at the same time the remedy, for our sorrows. From the moment that pain became the law of humanity, it also became the ladder to reclaim that Heaven from which sin had separated us. Pain became, after sin, the principal means of illuminating and giving meaning to the life of man.

6. The Sense of Pain in the Life of Man

Being a consequence of Original Sin, pain is evil perceived as such by perception and conscience. All creatures endowed with perception, animals and humans, feel physical evil, and from this feeling arises what is called suffering or pain. But

---

[245] St. Thomas Aquinas, *Summa Theologiae*, I–II, q. 79, a. 4, ad 1.

[246] F. Pollien, *La pianta di Dio*, cit., p. 155.

in animals, devoid of intelligence and will, pain stops at the sensory faculties. They suffer without being conscious of their pain. Man, endowed with intelligence and will, knows that he is suffering, and this increases his suffering. To the awareness of his material sufferings are added the properly moral sufferings, which tap directly into his soul. Moral sufferings are more intense and deeper than material sufferings and are characteristic of free and rational creatures, the only ones endowed with a spiritual and incorruptible soul.

Man, however, through his intelligence, can make sense of pain and understand that it is the consequence of sin, source of every evil in the universe. Irrational creatures suffer without the ability to give meaning to their suffering: men can understand the value of their pain even to the point of desiring it. St. Jane Francis de Chantal, who saw in pain the highest possibility of ascent to God given to man, said that she desired as a great grace "not even a single day of her life, indeed not even an hour, to be without pain."[247]

God is not pleased by the pain of men (Wisd. 1:13), whom He destined for happiness. In the plans of Divine Providence, man in the earthly Paradise, would pass from earthly life to heavenly life without being subject to death, to

---

[247] St. Jane Frances de Chantal, *Letter* n. 310.

deterioration, or to pain. Pain entered into the universal order of creation as a consequence of sin. From that moment on, it became the law of humanity, and no man can evade it.

"The history of pain," observes a keen Christian thinker, "is intrinsic in the history of humanity. Every milestone that man achieves walking through the deserted wasteland of the earth is a sorrowful station. Men are born and live in pain as birds in the air or fish in water. Pain is the element that men inhale and exhale. … Birth is the beginning of pain for man, living is the unending struggle with pain, death is pain which consumes existence. Human life, quickly fleeing, is a succession of pain; vanishing, is extreme pain."[248]

Physical evil or suffering resulting from sin can be a means of reparation or a source of merit when accepted with resignation and conformity to the divine will. For in suffering and in sin itself, God introduces for the sinner a possibility of good, granting him relief, if he repents and humbles himself, as is often the case. Nothing elevates man more than suffering freely accepted and courageously endured.

Furthermore, pain helps to judge life for what it is, stripping its outward appearances, and therefore helps to restore the truth of things; if the earth had no suffering, no

[248] N. Taccone-Gallucci, *L'uomo Dio*, cit., vol. II, p. 89.

pain, no catastrophes, it would exert an irresistible charm over us, we would not realize that it is a place of exile, and we would too easily forget that we are destined for Heaven.

It should not be forgotten that God is the master of life and death, measures out man's days on earth, and determines the manner of each person's death; that no man is innocent, because of Original Sin and present sins; that the greatest material evil is infinitely less than the least moral evil.

The moral evil of sin is often sought by men as good; physical evils, which are never true evils but can be valuable opportunities for purifying the soul and returning to God, are instead just as often evaded by men as irreparable and incomprehensible disasters. "Because of the faith that has languished in human hearts," says Pius XII, "because of the hedonism that informs and fascinates life, men are inclined to judge as evils, and absolute evils, all the physical misfortunes of this earth. They have forgotten that pain stands at the dawn of human life as a pathway to the smiles of the cradle; they have forgotten that more often than not it is a projection of the Cross of Calvary on the path of resurrection; they have forgotten that the cross is often a gift from God, a gift necessary to offer to divine justice our share of atonement as well; they have forgotten that the only real evil is the fault that offends God."[249]

---

[249] Pius XII, *Radio-message to the World,* June 29, 1941.

Suffering forces man to recognize what he is: a child of sin who does not renounce sin, "a blind and wounded beggar," as Ernest Hello defines him.[250] Forced, by admitting his own misery, to bow before God, he resembles Jesus Christ in this. "He who believes that he suffers without guilt," Father Zacchi writes, "let him never forget the Cross and the innocent victim of Calvary."[251]

7. Individual Evils and Collective Evils

God is not absent from history; on the contrary, He is always present in it with His boundlessness, and there is no point or moment in created time when divine justice and mercy is not manifested upon the peoples. All the disasters that befall nations in their history have purpose. Their causes sometimes elude us, but it is certain that the origin of all evil permitted by God lies in man's sin. St. Prosper of Aquitaine reminds us that "often the causes of divine work remain hidden and only the effects are seen."[252]

The greatness of Divine Providence is revealed not so much in the dispensation of graces intended to relieve the

---

[250] E. Hello, *Le più belle pagine*, tr. Ital. Orfanelli S. Cuore, Città di Castello 1927, p. 243.

[251] P. Angelo Zacchi, O.P., *Il problema del dolore*, Editrice Francesco Ferrari, Todi 1943, p. 213.

[252] St. Prosper of Aquitaine, *De vocatione omnium gentium*, tr. Ital. *La vocazione dei popoli*, Città Nuova, Roma 1998, p. 74.

material and moral woes of men, but above all in its ability to draw good from the physical and moral evil that is produced in the universe. God, who is entirely and only order, while in no way causing evil, gives any evil reason and meaning, transforming it into good for the creature that endures it.

Providence considers not only the good of individuals but also the common good of families, nations, and peoples to which the laws and sanctions attendant to them apply. After all, St. Thomas teaches, "in the same way that an individual person is punished for the sin he has committed because others refrain from sinning, so for some special sin a nation or a city may be punished because other peoples refrain from sinning."[253]

Joseph de Maistre, in his *St. Petersburg Dialogues*, reminds us of this fundamental truth: "a general law, if it is not unjust to all, cannot be unjust to the individual."[254] The just law is not that which has an effect on each individual, but rather the one that is made for all; its enforcement upon one man or another is entirely incidental. It is necessary to look at the law in its entirety before in its specific application in an individual case. For every law can have its exceptions, but the exceptions cannot make a law.

[253] St. Thomas Aquinas, *Summa Theologiae*, I–II, q. 105, a. 3, ad 1.
[254] J. de Maistre, *Le serate di San Pietroburgo*, Rusconi, Milano 1971, p. 22.

Evils of every kind, Maistre further notes, rain upon all mankind like bullets on an army, without any distinction between individuals, otherwise the miracle would become the ordinary condition of the world and would therefore itself cease to be a miracle.[255] It is necessary to accept them, because every man, in being a man, is subject to all the evils of humanity; the law is general, and therefore it is not "unjust."[256]

8. Particular Judgment and Universal Judgment

Justice, the theologians explain, is one of the infinite perfections of God.[257] Divine justice is the order of things in Heaven and on earth. The order by which everything gives glory to God and to Him alone and each thing attributed to Him has its place in creation.

The idea of justice, like that of divine justice, is often dismissed. Yet the doctrine of the Church teaches of the existence of a particular judgment that follows each person's death, with the immediate retribution of the soul, and of the universal judgment in which angels and men will be judged for their thoughts, words, acts, and

[255] Ibid., pp. 22–23.

[256] Ibid., p. 28.

[257] Réginald Garrigou-Lagrange, O.P., *Dieu, son existence et sa nature,* Beauchesne, Paris 1950, pp. 440–63.

omissions. For this reason, Scripture says: *Justus es Domine et rectum judicium tuum* (Ps. 119), "You are righteous, Lord, and just are your judgments."

God rewards all the good and punishes all the evil done by free creatures. What we call penance is the natural relationship that exists between fault and punishment.

Out of love, God allowed the moral evil of fault by giving man freedom, and out of love He willed that the physical evil of punishment be the necessary method of atonement. "Every punishment qua punishment," observes St. Bonaventure, "is just and comes from God. And no fault is just, nor does it come from God, but only from the free determination of the will."[258] The disordered will of man is the sole cause of the guilt of sin and of the punishment that the Lord wishes should follow it.

Fault lies within the essence of sin, and the corresponding punishment is proportionate to its gravity. Often, we understand the weight of the sin by the burden of the penance. If, for example, we did not know that Hell awaits unrepentant sinners, we would not understand the gravity of mortal sin, which is the singular true evil of the universe.

---

[258] St. Bonaventure, *Breviloquium*, parte III, cap. X, n. 1.

The infinite justice of God has its supreme manifestation in two different judgments that attend man at the end of his life: the particular judgment, to which every soul is subjected at the moment of death, and the universal judgment, to which all men will be subject, in body and soul, after the end of the world.

It is the belief of the Church that at the end of his own life, every man comes before God, Lord and supreme judge, to receive his reward or punishment. For this reason, Ecclesiasticus (Sirach) says: *Memor est judicii mei, sic enim erit et tuum* (Sir. 38), "Remember that his judgment will also be yours; for him it was yesterday, for you today."

In the particular judgment, explains Fr. Garrigou-Lagrange, the soul spiritually understands that it is judged by God and under the divine light his conscience speaks the same divine judgment. "This happens in the first instant the soul is separated from the body, such that it is just as true to say that a person is dead as to say that he is judged."[259] The sentence is definitive and the execution of the sentence is instantaneous and final.

But the second judgment awaits us after death: the universal judgment. St. Thomas explains the reason for this:

[259] R. Garrigou-Lagrange, *La vita eterna e la profondità dell'anima*, tr. Ital., *Fede e Cultura*, Verona 2018, p. 94.

> Each man is a person in himself and is at the
> same time part of the whole human race; for
> this reason, he is owed a double judgment: the
> particular one, after his death when he will re-
> ceive according to what he did in life, though
> not entirely as he will not receive as to the body,
> but as to the soul; but there must be another
> judgment according to our part in the human
> race: The universal judgment of the whole
> human race, by means of the universal separa-
> tion of the good from the bad.[260]

The Angelic Doctor explains in another passage that even though the temporal life of man ends with death, it is in some way prolonged into the future because the man continues to live on in the memory of other men, beginning with his children. Moreover, the life of man continues in the effects of his works. For example, St. Thomas says, "from the fraud of Arian and the other imposters unbelief effervesces until the end of time, and until that end, the faith will be spread by the strength of the preaching of the apostles."[261]

God's judgment extends until the end of time because until then the good influence of the saints or the bad

[260] Thomas Aquinas, *In IV Sent.* 47, 1, 1, ad 1.
[261] Id., *Summa Theologiae*, III, q. 59, art. 5.

influence of the reprobate can extend over the earth. The existence of a universal judgment, which follows the particular judgment, is a proposition of faith. St. Augustine distills the teaching of the Church in these words: "No one doubts or denies that Jesus Christ will pronounce the last judgment just as Holy Scripture announces it."[262]

9. God's Judgment in History

The particular judgment and the universal judgment are the two highest moments in which God's judgment upon men and upon the nations is made manifest. Following this divine judgment is reward or punishment. But to men, the reward or punishment can apply during their lives or after death (and thereafter for eternity), while for nations, which do not have eternal life, the reward or punishment can come to pass only throughout history.

Wicked men can enjoy wealth in their temporal life because their fate is nevertheless sealed in eternity. Their temporal prosperity is the earthly reward of their few good deeds, though they cannot be rewarded in the afterlife because evil has prevailed in them. The wicked nations who, in contrast to individuals, have no eternal life, are destined to

---

[262] St. Augustine, *De Civitate Dei*, 20, 30.

pay off their debts in time and history. God is just and remunerative, and gives to each his own: He does not punish or reward only individual people, but also afflicts families, cities, and nations for the sins they commit. So says Sirach, "[To sinners] come plague and bloodshed, fiery heat and drought, plunder and ruin, famine and death. For the wicked evil was created, and because of them destruction hastens" (Sir. 40:9–10).

Pope Pius XII teaches that though the Lord "often punishes private individuals for their sins only after death, nonetheless, as history teaches, He occasionally punishes in this mortal life rulers of people and their nations when they have dealt unjustly with others. For He is a just judge."[263] The sin of society as a whole is far more serious than the sins of the individual men that compose it, for the same reason that the common good of citizens is far greater than their individual good acts. And since the punishment corresponds to the sins, the theology of Christian history teaches us that great catastrophes are often the punishments that serve to pay off the public sins of nations. Throughout these catastrophes, God's justice is never separate from His mercy, but the mercy of God is

---

[263] Pius XII, Enc. *Datis Nuperrime*, November 5, 1956.

tied to repentance, and punishment becomes inevitable when society, by refusing both repentance and penance, calls down upon itself not God's mercy, but His justice.

Earthquakes, famines, epidemics, wars, and revolutions have always been considered divine punishment: *A fame, peste, et bello libera nos Domine* (Deliver us, Lord, from famine, plague, and war) is the liturgical invocation that has been repeated throughout the centuries on Rogation days or in the processions proclaimed by the Church to implore Heaven's help against those disasters that the Christian people have always understood as punishments. *Tria sunt flagella quibus Dominus castigat*: "There are three scourges that the Lord uses to chastise His people: war, pestilence, and famine," warned St. Bernardino of Siena.[264] With these three scourges, he explains, God punishes the three principal vices of man: pride, lust, and avarice — pride, when the soul rebels against God (Rev. 12:7–9); lust, when the body rebels against the soul (Gen. 6:5–7); avarice, when things rebel against man (Ps. 97:3). War is the punishment against the pride of the people, plague is

[264] St. Bernardino of Siena, *Sermo XLVI, Feria quinta post dominicam de Passione*, in *Opera omnia*, Ad Claras Aquas, Florentiae 1950, vol. II, pp. 84–85.

the punishment against their lust, and famine is the punishment against their avarice.

St. Bernardino adds to this that the closer God's punishment is, the less the people who deserve it will recognize it.[265] The reason for their mind's blindness is pride — *initium omnis peccati*, "the origin of every sin" (Sir. 10:15). Pride darkens the intellect, obscuring how near to ruin the sinner is, and by blinding him God wishes to humble the proud.

Furthermore, God "often chastises one sin with other sins and does so justly" as a result of the obstinance and pride of the sinner, writes Fr. Ribadaneira.[266] "A terrible punishment to be feared beyond any punishment," he adds. For "neither drought, nor famine, nor corrupt and contaminated air, nor plague, nor war, nor revolution of kingdoms, nor any other disaster that there is, no matter how grave, is so frightful a sign of divine wrath, of the fury of God, as this scourge of sin heaped upon sin; For, no matter how grave the first sins may be, nevertheless they are a punishment of the Father, but this is the punishment and vengeance of the enemy."[267]

[265] Id., *Sermo XIX, Feria secunda post II dominicam in quadragesima*, in *Opera Omnia*, cit., vol. III, pp. 340–50.

[266] Pietro Ribadaneira S.J., *La tribolazione e i suoi conforti*, Civiltà Cattolica, Roma 1914, pp. 228–29.

[267] Ibid., p. 230.

10. The Sin of Lucifer and the Rebellious Angels

The Original Sin of Adam and Eve is the root of all physical evils and all sins of man, but there was, in the history of the universe, a sin even more serious and horrible than Original Sin: the sin of Lucifer and of the rebellious angels, committed before God just a moment after the creation of time.

At the dawn of Creation, the angelic spirits knew perfectly, with only a glance, their most pure nature, and they saw instantaneously their intimate dependence upon God, the singular good of the universe. There is a profound mystery in the opening event of the history of the universe, a tragic question that since that moment has echoed throughout time: "How, O Lucifer, did you fall from Heaven, who were born at dawn?" (Isa. 14:12). And Scripture itself suggests the reasons for the angelic sin, when it says, "Your heart had grown haughty because of your beauty; You corrupted your wisdom because of your splendor" (Ezek. 28:17). In the moment Lucifer was satisfied with himself alone, turning his sight from the source of his own being and its perfection, he tore his will from the highest good, and he hated it with irrevocable animosity by virtue of the strength of his will which froze in a state of hatred for eternity. "The fall is for the angels what death is for men," writes St. Thomas, citing St. John Damascene. "There is no possibility of repentance for them after the fall, just as there is no possibility of repentance for man after death."[268]

The angelic sin was a boundless sin of pride.[269] The devil wished to be like God, even if he did not wish to be entirely the same as God, as St. Anselm explains, because that which he wanted, he wanted against God's will, and therefore he wished to be similar to God, but in a disordered manner, because he wished for something of his own will, without submitting his will to anyone else: "For to will something of one's own will, without obedience to any higher will, must be the privilege only of God."[270] The sin of the angels was the first and highest sin, by virtue of their preeminent nature as the purest spirits, capable of intuitive understanding and immediate self-determination, but also capable of sinning and retreating from God as contingent and free creatures. The greater part of the angels adored God and the future Christ, but Lucifer rebelled, and with him "a third of the stars in the sky" (Rev. 12:4). *Proelium factum est in coelis* "Then war broke out in

---

[268] St. Thomas Aquinas, *Summa Theologiae*, I, q. 64, a. 2; St. John Damascene, *De fide orthodoxa*, lib. II, cap. IV; PG, t. XCIV, col. 877.

[269] Id., *Summa Theologiae,* I, q. 63, a. 2.

[270] St. Anselm of Canterbury, *La caduta del diavolo*, cit., p. 73.

Heaven," (Rev. 12:7). From one end of the created Heaven to the other a momentous battle commenced which lasted perhaps only the length of a shout: The *"quis ut Deus"* levied against Lucifer by the Archangel Michael, prince of the heavenly armies ever since.

In the universe of light that is Heaven, a horrific pit of darkness opened wide. The abyss swallowed up the rebellious angels. The upward movement that thrust the angels toward God transformed into an irresistible whirlpool that cast them down forever "among the dark abysses of Hell" (2 Peter 2:4), "prepared for the devil and his angels" (Matt. 25:41). St. John, in Revelation, speaks of the abyss of which Satan is king (9:11) because he possesses the key to it (9:1). An angel will cast Satan back into his chasm and will hermetically seal the cavity so that he will no longer deceive people (20:1–3).

11. The Two Flags Flown in the Universe

At the root of Lucifer's sin, like every sin, is pride, *amor excellentiae propriae*, as St. Augustine defines it,[271] the disordered love of self in opposition to the well-ordered love of God. The force of attraction and cohesion that generates and

---

[271] St. Augustine, *De Genesi ad Litteram*, XI, 14, 18.

maintains them is love: "Two loves have created two cities: one earthly by love of self to the point of contempt of God; the heavenly one by love of God to the point of contempt of self."[272] The fundamental choice is between God, to whom humility of heart intimately unites us, and the devil, to whom pride and love of self bind us. The essence of this clash is moral and rooted in human freedom: we must choose according to the pull that love imprints on our lives.[273]

In these two opposite directions of love every human life unfolds: either toward God, to whom humility intimately unites us, which is the love of truth and goodness, or toward the devil, to whom pride beyond measure binds us irrevocably.

In his encyclical against Freemasonry of April 20, 1884, *Humanum genus*, Leo XIII asserts:

> The race of man, after its miserable fall from God, the Creator and the Giver of heavenly gifts, 'through the envy of the devil,' separated into two diverse and opposite parts, of which the one steadfastly contends for truth and virtue, the other of those things which are contrary to virtue and to truth. The one is the kingdom of God on

---

[272] Id., *De Civitate Dei*, lib. XIV, c. 28.

[273] Msgr. Antonino Romeo, *Il presente e il futuro nella Rivelazione biblica*, Descléee, Rome 1964, pp. 1–32.

earth, namely, the true Church of Jesus Christ; and those who desire from their heart to be united with it, so as to gain salvation, must of necessity serve God and His only-begotten Son with their whole mind and with an entire will. The other is the kingdom of Satan, in whose possession and control are all whosoever follow the fatal example of their leader and of our first parents, those who refuse to obey the divine and eternal law, and who have many aims of their own in contempt of God, and many aims also against God.

In order to explain this mystery of iniquity, Leo XIII recalls the two cities that St. Augustine describes in the following words: "One is the society of devout men, the other of the rebellious, each with the angels belonging to it, in which in the former the love of God is superior, in the other love of self."[274]

The *Spiritual Exercises* of St. Ignatius remind us of the military attitude of the Christian, who is called to choose between two flags, which stand for none other than the two cities of which St. Augustine speaks.[275] St. Ignatius and St. Augustine merely make explicit the Gospel maxim "No

---

[274] St. Augustine, *De Civitate Dei*, lib. XIV, c. 13,1.

[275] St. Ignatius of Loyola, *Esercizi Spirituali*, nn. 136–138, tr. Ital. a cura del padre Giovanni Filippo Roothan S.J., Editrice Ancora, Milano 1967, pp. 166–69.

one can serve two masters. He will either hate one and love the other, or be devoted to one and despise the other" (Matt. 6:24; Luke 16:13). Our life is a moment in this struggle, which is the story of total war between the servants of the order of God and the followers of infernal chaos. Two shouts echo, like the two flags, from the beginning of time: the one turns the "I" of the creature, which is nothingness, into the whole of the universe; the other proclaims God as the first cause and ultimate end of creation. "*Non serviam*" or "*Quis ut Deus*": one is a shout of pride, the other a proclamation of humility. A denial of unfathomable blindness and an assertion of resplendent logic. An insatiable impulse of hatred and a surge of unquenchable love. From these two declarations descends the moral dualism of the universe, the fundamental incompatibility between the good and the evil that is opposed to it.

All the good that has its cause in God and all the evil that though not caused by God is permitted by Him — in short, all the good and evil destined to oppose each other in history — derive from this primordial struggle. Every good in God's plans, however, precedes this event because it was conceived *ab aeterno* by Divine Wisdom, while every evil descends from creatures and is successive to the beginning of created time.

12. The *Mysterium Iniquitatis* in History

The moral evil that St. Paul defines as *mysterium iniquitatis* (2 Thess. 2:7), is a terrible and profound mystery. This mystery, the opening event of history, reveals itself in the Passion of Jesus Christ and will be made manifest with growing intensity until the last day of the world.

Evil in history can grow and develop, but it has insurmountable limits: it is unable to undo the effects of the Redemption, nor can it overcome the Church. Nevertheless, it can expand in depth and breadth, so much so as to give a reason for the question in the Gospel: "When the Son of Man comes, will he find faith on earth?" (Luke 18:8).

The rule of the antichrist will be the foremost expression of evil in history, the most terrible form of persecution: that which prefers apostates to martyrs. It is foretold by the Apostle in these words: "For ... the apostasy comes first and the lawless one is revealed, the one doomed to perdition, who opposes and exalts himself above every so-called god and object of worship, so as to seat himself in the temple of God, claiming that he is a god" (2 Thess. 2:3–4).

The age of the apostasy of the antichrist will be a reign of chaos and darkness upon the earth. On that day, Satan will rule over the world (Rev. 9:20) and the empire of evil will expand to such an extent that it will not be possible to hide from the essential choice for Jesus Christ or against Him. There can be no neutrality among the camps, just as there was none in the moment of the creation of the angels. There will be no opportunity to hide, no chance of exile. "The fronts will be differentiated so clearly," writes Fr. Schmaus, "that no one could remain outside of the struggle. There will be no possibility of flight: no one will be able to escape."[276]

The persecution of Christians and the defection of many of them from the struggle will culminate in those days, which will see a "great tribulation, such as has not been since the beginning of the world until now, nor ever will be" (Matt. 24:21). Nevertheless, the Lord will not permit the darkness of the Great Apostasy to cover the world over before the light of the Gospel has shined upon all its peoples (Matt. 24:14). The enormity of the scandal in the last days of the world, adds Fr. Calmel, will not diminish the power of the Lord, such that for the Christians who will live in that time, there will be no true reason to lose courage nor to lack confidence in victory.[277]

The mystery of evil, which will reach its apex in the time of the antichrist, has its roots in the freedom of the

---

[276] M. Schmaus, *Dogmatica cattolica*, cit., vol. IV/1, p. 176.

[277] P. Roger T. Calmel O.P., *Teologia della storia*, Borla, Torino 1967, p. 106.

creature called to unite itself to the divine will or to irreparably separate from it. This mystery is no different from the mystery of love that God will manifest toward His elect when in the last days they will defy the persecutions and torments in order to fight the antichrist.

The upheaval of the last days of the world is not a scandal to our faith in the divine love, since we are sure that Satan is conquered from the very beginning and cooperates, against his will, for the greater glory of God. Christ, with the unsurpassed fullness of His light and grace, remains with us each day and makes the ages endure so that we may participate in His Passion and victory.[278] At the end of time, when the number of martyrs will be complete, at the height of the persecution of the antichrist, He will finally appear triumphant in His Parousia (Rev. 6:11).

13. The Sin of Revolution

Between the sin of Lucifer, which opened it, and that of the antichrist, which will conclude it, the history of evil has been and continues to be quite familiar with the attempt to distort the divine order, driving men and their society from their one and highest good.

[278] Ibid., p. 140.

The glory of God is the aim and end of all the universe; man and angel, inanimate and living beings, the spiritual order and the temporal one, in its every expression, do not evade this duty. In the social order, man must recognize the image of divine perfection.[279] If human society does not render glory to God, it sins, and it sins as deeply as it departs from God in its customs and laws.

The sin of society as a whole is far more serious than the sins of the individual men that compose it for the same reason that the common good of citizens is greater than their individual goods. For a collection of souls reflects more perfectly the glory of God or expresses in a more distorted manner its departure from Him. There exists, in this sense, a "common evil," analogous and contrary to the common good of the universe. It has its roots in the *aversio a Deo* (turning away from God), in the retreat of society as a whole from God.

True disorder in society is not its instability or conflict, which can arise among its members, but the turning away from God outside of whom peace does not exist and order is not possible. This deep social disorder can be understood as revolution, because every revolution is the subversion of an order: in this case, the order that is being

---

[279] Pius XI, Enc. *Divini Redemptoris,* March 19, 1937, in Denz-H n. 3772.

subverted is not simply a factual order, but the order qua order, that is the divine disposition of things made within time, in the image of the heavenly hierarchy in eternity. This revolutionary disorder is produced and can only be produced by rational creatures — men and fallen angels — because only these, insofar as they are free beings, can resist God and turn away from the model of order that He has imprinted on the universe.

Revolution, unfolding in history, has in turn a cause and an archetype in the first revolution that unfolded from the beginning of time: the rebellion of Lucifer against the divine plan of the universe.

The seed of revolution is hatred toward God and toward the hierarchical disposition of creation willed by Divine Providence. This hatred expresses itself in the form of metaphysical denial of the order of the universe. "The essence of the revolutionary spirit," writes Plinio Corrêa de Oliveira, "consists in hating on principle and on the metaphysical level any inequality and any law, especially the moral law."[280]

Revolution, throughout history, has seen explosions of hate and fury such as Protestantism, the French Revolution

---

[280] P. Corrêa de Oliveira, *Rivoluzione e Contro-Rivoluzione*, tr. Ital. Sugarco, Milano 2009, p. 130.

and its Communist counterparts, or the totalitarianism and anarchy of the twentieth century; but its historical origins arise from the loss of Christian faith and spirit that characterized the decline of Medieval Christendom, when humanism and the Renaissance signaled the beginning of a progressive retreat from God in the institutions and customs of European society. "The heart," writes Monsignor Delassus, "was no longer to love God, the mind to know Him, the body to serve Him, and in so doing to merit eternal life."[281]

This revolution, asserts Plinio Corrêa de Oliveira, is a process that was "born in a given moment with great intensity in the deepest parts of the soul and culture of Western man. It is a long system of causes and effects that would go on to produce successive convulsions from the fifteenth century through to today."[282] Its driving force is in the unfettered human passions, a consequence of Original Sin. The same author shows how, from the deepest parts of the soul, the revolutionary crisis moved into trends, ideological positions, and ultimately into the realm of facts, extending progressively in depth and breadth into all the world. Contemporary chaos

---

[281] Mons. Henri Delassus, *Il problema dell'ora presente*, tr. Ital. Desclée, Roma 1907, vol. I, p. 57.

[282] P. Corrêa de Oliveira, *Rivoluzione e Contro-Rivoluzione*, cit., pp. 46–47.

is the culmination of more than five centuries of apostasy and rejection of the rights of God over society. Chaos and destructive nihilism are its ultimate logical result.

14. The Diabolic Character of Revolution

Revolution is the retreat of people and society from God: an *aversio a Deo* that develops over time with a growing intensity and with persistent stubbornness: in this sense it is diabolical. Revolution is, in its essence, satanic because it constitutes a series of events designed to take the rights of God over human society away from Him and transfer them to the devil.

The devil remains the principal architect of revolution, but he needs the cooperation of men to operate within history. Revolution is born and develops thanks to this cooperation with evil acting in opposition to those righteous ones cooperating with divine grace; it is the creation within history of a mystical "body" that stands against that of the Redeemer, with Lucifer as its head, just as the mystical body of the Church has Jesus Christ as her head and the Most Holy Mary as her Mother. "The devil," asserts St. Gregory the Great, "is in fact the head of all wicked people and these are the members of the body to which he is the head."[283] "It is a doctrine of

---

[283] St. Gregory the Great, *Lectio Sancti Evangelii secundum Matthaeum*, Hom. XVI, 1.

faith," writes Fr. Scheeben, "that humanity, by the sin of Adam, became a prisoner and slave of the devil.... The *mysterium iniquitatis* within humanity is made manifest in the all too clear lordship of the devil over the creature, more powerfully even than the sway that concupiscence holds."[284]

Revolution is not the transgression of divine law in one spot, but the denial of this law in itself. What's more, it is the rejection of the benefits of the Redemption, assured by the Holy Spirit through the work of the Church; it is the rejection of Christian civilization, daughter of the Church and the sacrifice on Calvary. Revolution is the expression of sin and disorder in its chief form, the proclamation of chaos as the founding principle of reality, of total disorder as the singular "pseudo-order" of the universe.

"The revolution," Donoso Cortés states, "is the ultimate end to which pride has arrived."[285] "The earth," writes Msgr. Delassus, "has not yet seen anything more deeply unjust than the revolution. It does not come from any passion, but from pride, the origin of every evil, especially when it rises up against God; it is not an error, but the fundamental error, that which prevails against God Himself,

---

[284] J. Scheeben, *I misteri del cristianesimo*, cit., p. 231.
[285] J. Donoso Cortés, *Pensamientos varios* in *Obras*, Bac, Madrid 1970, vol. II, p. 980.

the foundation of every truth and good; it is not an evil, but the evil; it is satanic in its essence."[286]

Revolution is not only a sin, but it is the worst of all sins after Lucifer's *non serviam* because it represents its expression and continuation throughout time. "The revolution," asserts once again Donoso Cortés, "is not only a crime, but the greatest of all crimes, because it is crime par excellence."[287]

If crime is indeed the violation par excellence of the law, no worse crime can be imagined than the premeditated and organized rejection of the eternal law, i.e., the rejection of the plan eternally and unchangeably established by Divine Providence for men and society. Revolution is an immense evil because it spreads and intensifies the burden of sin, the singular true evil of the universe, within history.

To the Lord who says of Himself, "I am the One who is" (Exod. 3:14), Satan, head and soul of the revolution, shouts: "Nothing is outside of me and I hate because I am." The devil would like to plunge creation into nothingness and to cast himself into nothingness. The *mysterium iniquitatis* is the mystery of the pull of evil toward nothingness, without

[286] Msgr. H. Delassus, *Il problema dell'ora presente*, cit., vol. II, p. 43.
[287] J. Donoso Cortés, *Historia de la Regencia de Maria Cristina*, in *Obras*, cit., vol. I, p. 935.

being able to reach this goal. If this total suicide could not be enacted, the revolution would have prevailed over God, seeing as annihilation is the supreme act of dominion, possible only to God,[288] but also because evil exists only in the deprivation of the good,[289] and without the good it cannot exist, just as disease cannot exist without the body of the sick man that it attacks. Death means the end not only of the sick man, but also of the sickness that afflicts him.

For this reason, the revolution's journey to nowhere cannot reach its end: the radical and definitive destruction of the Church and Christian civilization. That good which remains and upon which the revolution relies in order to survive is the root of its demise.

15. *Inimicitias Ponam*

"A world with evil," writes Cardinal Journet, "can be better, in its entirety, than a world without evil because it can arouse allegiances, repentances, and loves that a world over which the most terrible storms did not rage would ignore forever."[290] To the extent that evil infiltrates the world, divine mercy becomes

[288] St. Thomas Aquinas, *Summa Theologiae*, I–IIae, q. 84, ad 3; id., I, q. 104, a. 3.

[289] Ibid., I, q. 14, a. 10, resp.

[290] Card. C. Journet, *Per una teologia della storia della salvezza*, cit., p. 134.

more abundant. For St. Paul writes, "God has closed all men with disobedience in order to do mercy to all" (Rom. 11:32). God brings boundless good from immeasurable evil. The angelic rebellion is the source and consequence not only of the Incarnation of the Word, but of Divine Motherhood itself and therefore of the privileged role of Mary, who will be the one to crush the head of the devil and to bring the plans of God in history to their perfect fulfillment.

Before it is time, in the decrees of Divine Wisdom, the absolutely pure and perfectly humble heart of Mary stands in opposition to the heart of the fallen Angel, swollen with impiety and pride and an abyss of every sort of evil. By the will of God, the pride of Lucifer will not be crushed directly by divine power, but by the unfathomable humility of a creature in whom God has placed, by His love, all of His power.[291]

God wanted a simple creature like Mary to oppose the devil in order to remind us that Satan should not be considered in the same way as God. For he, too, is a creature, and therefore subject to the Creator: he is the prince of this world (John 12:31, 14:30, 16:11), but the lordship that he exercises over the world is permitted by God, who is its true and only master, so that the divine glory may better stand out.

[291] St. Louis-Marie Grignion de Montfort, *Trattato della Vera Devozione*, n. 52.

The books of Genesis and Revelation, which open and close Sacred Scripture, offer us words and images that the Fathers and Doctors of the Church, saints and theologians, have meditated upon over the course of the centuries. In Genesis, the Lord says: "I will put enmity between you and the woman, and between your offspring and hers; They will strike at your head, while you strike at their heel" (Gen. 3:15). The twelfth chapter of Revelation describes the furious struggle of the infernal dragon against the offspring of the Virgin. The immaculate woman appears clothed with the sun, with the moon beneath her feet and a crown of twelve stars upon her head; before her stands the Dragon tinged red with the blood of the martyrs, proud and ferocious, seemingly invincible, but destined for a final defeat (Rev. 12:1–8).

The only enmity created by God, yet irreconcilable and which will last, or rather even increase until the end of time, explains St. Louis-Marie Grignion de Montfort, is that between Mary and the devil; between the sons and servants of the Most Blessed Virgin and the sons and followers of Lucifer.[292] One creature, the devil, presumed to warp the work of creation. To another creature, Providence

[292] Ibid.

has permitted to restore that disfigured divine order in all its truth and beauty. The devil is the father of sin, chaos, and the revolution; our Lady is the Mother of every grace, every order, and every restoration.

Inimicitas ponam: "This sentence," writes Msgr. Delassus, "connects the history of the earth with the history of Heaven. The first command of a war that would end among us took place in Heaven above."[293] The battle between the angels is the prototype of every battle throughout history. The cosmic history, from the beginning until the end of time, is the history of this total war between the servants of the order of God and the infernal chaos. In this war, the victory of God is decided from the moment in which the devil, like a bolt of lightning, plunged irreversibly from Heaven (Luke 10:17). This battle and this victory in Heaven prefigures a battle and victory on the earth between the offspring of Mary and that of Lucifer: it is the victory that will establish Mary's Kingdom.

---

[293] Msgr. H. Delassus, *Il problema dell'ora presente*, cit., vol. II, p. 41.

About the Author

ROBERTO DE MATTEI IS a Catholic historian who has taught in several Italian universities. Between 2003 and 2011, he served as vice president of the National Research Council, the highest Italian scientific institution. He is president of the Lepanto Foundation and is the editor of the magazine *Radici Cristiane* and the news agency Corrispondenza Romana. He is the author of thirty-five books, including *The Second Vatican Council: An Unwritten Story* (2011), translated into eight languages, and *Love for the Papacy & Filial Resistance to the Pope in the History of the Church* (2019). He has received many awards, including membership in the Order of St. Gregory the Great from the Holy See for his service to the Roman Catholic Church. He is married with five children.

Sophia Institute

Sophia Institute is a nonprofit institution that seeks to nurture the spiritual, moral, and cultural life of souls and to spread the Gospel of Christ in conformity with the authentic teachings of the Roman Catholic Church.

Sophia Institute Press fulfills this mission by offering translations, reprints, and new publications that afford readers a rich source of the enduring wisdom of mankind.

Sophia Institute also operates the popular online Catholic resource CatholicExchange.com. *Catholic Exchange* provides world news from a Catholic perspective as well as daily devotionals and articles that will help readers to grow in holiness and live a life consistent with the teachings of the Church.

In 2013, Sophia Institute launched Sophia Institute for Teachers to renew and rebuild Catholic culture through service to Catholic education. With the goal of nurturing the spiritual, moral, and cultural life of souls, and an abiding respect for the role and work of teachers, we strive to provide materials and programs that are at once enlightening to the mind and ennobling to the heart; faithful and complete, as well as useful and practical.

Sophia Institute gratefully recognizes the Solidarity Association for preserving and encouraging the growth of our apostolate over the course of many years. Without their generous and timely support, this book would not be in your hands.

www.SophiaInstitute.com
www.CatholicExchange.com
www.SophiaInstituteforTeachers.org

Sophia Institute Press® is a registered trademark of Sophia Institute.
Sophia Institute is a tax-exempt institution as defined by the
Internal Revenue Code, Section 501(c)(3). Tax I.D. 22-2548708.